SCIENCE OF SUCCESSFUL SELLING

NAPOLEON
HILL'S

SCIENCE OF SUCCESSFUL SELLING

NAPOLEON HILL
ASSOCIATES

Published 2020 by Gildan Media LLC
aka G&D Media
www.GandDmedia.com

NAPOLEON HILL'S SCIENCE OF SUCCESSFUL SELLING. Copyright ©2020
by The Napoleon Hill Foundation. All rights reserved.

Front Cover design by David Rheinhardt of Pyrographx

Interior design by Meghan Day Healey of Story Horse, LLC

Library of Congress Cataloging-in-Publication Data is available upon
request

ISBN: 978-1-7225-0309-3

10   9   8   7   6   5   4   3   2   1

Contents

Chapter Five

Chapter Six

Chapter Seven

Chapter Eight

Chapter Nine

Chapter Ten

Chapter Eleven

Chapter One

THE PRINCIPLES OF
PRACTICAL PSYCHOLOGY USED
IN SUCCESSFUL NEGOTIATION

The ability to influence people without irritating them is the most profitable art known to humanity. This entire book is devoted to an analysis of the accepted principles of psychology, through which anyone may negotiate with others without friction.

These are the only known principles by which one may win friends and influence people without unnecessarily flattering them. The principles were organized from the life experiences of some of the most successful leaders in business industry, finance, and education known to the American people in the first half of the twentieth century. In this book, one may find modern salesmanship in its most fitting, streamlined clothes.

Professional salespeople are artists who can paint word pictures in the hearts of others as skillfully as Rembrandt could blend colors on a canvas. They are artists who can play symphonies on the human emotions as effectively as Paderewski could manipulate the keys of a piano. Professional salespeople are strategists at mind manipulation; they can marshal the thoughts of others as ably as Eisenhower directed the Allied armies during World War II.

Professional salespeople are philosophers who can interpret causes by their effects and effects by their causes. They are character analysts; they know people as Einstein knew higher mathematics. They are mind readers. They know what thoughts are in other people's minds by the expressions on their faces, by the words they utter, by their silence, and by the feeling the salesperson experiences in their presence.

Professional salespeople are fortune tellers. They can predict the future by observing what has happened in the past. They are masters of others, because they are masters of themselves.

The attributes of professional selling will be described in this book, as well as the means by which these qualities may be acquired. This book's purpose is to enable the reader to transform mediocrity into professionalism in the art of persuasion.

Life is a series of ever changing and shifting circumstances and experiences. No two experiences are alike. No two people are alike. Day after day, we experience life's kaleidoscopic changes. This makes it necessary for us to adapt ourselves to people who think and act in ways different from our own. Our success depends largely upon how well we negotiate our way through these daily contacts with other people without friction or opposition. This sort of negotiation calls for an understanding of the art of salesmanship. We are all salespeople regardless of our calling, although not all of us are *professional* salespeople.

Politicians must sell their way into office. If they are to remain in office, they must keep themselves sold to their constituents. Salaried people must sell themselves into a job. Salesmanship must be used to keep the position after it has been obtained. Anyone who seeks a loan in a bank must sell the banker on making the loan. Clergy must sell their sermons, and themselves as well, to their followers. If they do a poor job, they soon find themselves looking for another call. Lawyers must sell the merits of their clients' cases to the judge and jury, even if they know the case has but little merit. If a man chooses to marry, he must sell himself to the woman of his choice (albeit the woman may and often does remove many of the obstacles in the path of the sale). Laborers must sell themselves to employers, although the form of salesmanship required is not as difficult as that which must be employed by those who sell themselves into job at top-level salaries. These are examples of salesmanship through which people sell intangibles.

Any form of effort through which one person persuades another to cooperate is salesmanship. Most efforts at salesmanship are weak, and for this reason most people are poor salespeople. If someone attains a high station in life, it is because they have acquired or have been blessed with native ability in sales. Schooling, college degrees, intellect, and brilliance are of no avail to those who lack the ability to attract the cooperative efforts of others and thus to create opportunities for themselves. These qualities help individuals to make the most of opportunities, but they must first create these opportunities. Perhaps by the law of averages, opportunity is thrust upon one out of every hundred thousand people; the others must create opportunity.

Salesmanship is often as necessary in the development of opportunity as in its creation. Salesmanship, as described in this book, does not apply only to marketing commodities and services. You can sell your personality; indeed, you must. As a matter of fact, the major object of this book is to teach men and women how to sell their way through life successfully, using the selling strategy and the psychology used by the professional salesperson in selling goods and services.

During his youth, Herbert Hoover was handicapped by the loss of his parents. Millions of other orphans have lived and died without having had the opportunity to make themselves known outside their local communities. What distinguishing features did Mr. Hoover possess to enable him to set his sights in the direction of the White House and ride with fortune to that high goal? He discovered how to sell his way through life successfully.

This course is intended to teach others to do the same. One author has given five definitions of salesmanship:

1. Selling is the ability to make known your goods, services, or propositions to a person or persons to the point of creating a desire for a privilege, opportunity, possession, or an interest.

2. Selling is the ability of professional and public individuals to render services, assistance, and cooperation to the point of creating a desire on the part of people to remunerate, recognize, and honor.

3. Selling is the ability to perform work duties and services as an employee to the point of creating a desire on the part of an employer to remunerate, promote, and praise.

4. Selling is the ability to be polite, kind, agreeable, and considerate to the point of creating a desire on the part of those you meet to respect, love, and honor you.

5. Selling is the ability to write, design, paint, invent, create, compose, or accomplish anything to the point of creating a desire on the part of people to acclaim its possessors as heroes, celebrities, and people of greatness.

These definitions are very broad; they cover a great variety of all human activity. The whole of any life is one long, unbroken chain of sales endeavors. The newly born babe is a salesperson: when it wants food, it yells for it and gets it. When it is in pain, it yells for attention and gets that too. Women are the greatest salespeople on earth. They are often more subtle and more dramatic and use greater finesse than men. Men often believe they are selling themselves to women in proposals of marriage. Generally, however, it is the woman who does the selling. She does it by making herself charming, attractive, and alluring.

While these definitions are comprehensive, we could add to this list one more: selling is the art of planting in the mind of another a motive that will induce favorable action. The importance of this definition will be apparent throughout this book.

A salesperson becomes a professional salesperson because of his or her ability to induce other people to act upon motives without resistance or friction. There is little competition among professional salespeople, because there are so few of them.

Professional salespeople know what they want, and they know how to plan the acquisition of it. Moreover, they have the initiative to put such a plan into action.

There are two forms of sales endeavor: when the salesperson is negotiating with only one person and when he or she is negotiating with a group of people. The latter is commonly known as group selling or public speaking. The professional salesperson's education is not complete unless they have the ability to persuade groups of people as well as individuals.

The ability to speak to groups with a force that carries conviction is a priceless asset. It has given many people their biggest opportunity. This ability must be self-acquired. It is an art that can be acquired only through study, effort, and experience. Here are some specific instances.

William Jennings Bryan lifted himself from obscurity to a position of national prominence through his famous Cross of Gold speech during the Democratic convention of 1896.

Patrick Henry immortalized himself through his famous "Give me liberty or give me death" speech in the days of the American Revolution. But for that speech, his name might never have achieved renown.

Robert Ingersoll changed the trend of theology by his eloquent art and forceful group salesmanship.

One of the most effective lessons in salesmanship ever written is in Shakespeare's masterpiece: Mark Antony's speech at the funeral of Julius Caesar.

John F. Kennedy will always be remembered for this line: "Think not what your country can do for you, but what you can do for your country."

The professional salesperson has the ability to influence people through the printed page as well as by the spoken word. Elbert Hubbard accumulated a modest fortune and indelibly impressed his name upon the minds of men through the selling power of his pen. Perhaps Thomas Paine, through the power of his pen, did more than anyone else to inspire the American Revolution. Benjamin Franklin immortalized himself and left his imprint for good upon civilization by the forceful simplicity and quaintness of his written salesmanship. Abraham Lincoln immortalized himself through a single speech: his Gettysburg Address—simple in theme, pure in composition, moving in thought. Albert Schweitzer, philosopher, theologian, musician, medical missionary, and winner of a Nobel Peace Prize, dedicated his life to selling his personal philosophy: respect for the lives of other beings and the demand for the highest development of an individual's resources.

Caesar, Alexander, Napoleon, Hitler, Castro, and hundreds of others of their type were also professional salesmen, but they built their sales presentations around motives that were destructive of the best impulses of civilization. They sold and delivered wars—wars for which the people paid in blood and tears and suffering. Enduring success and selling is always predicated upon sound motive. Remember this, you who aspire to mastery in selling: sell neither stones nor serpents nor swords.

The world now faces the greatest opportunity for professional salesmanship in history. New leaders and a new brand of leadership are needed throughout the world in almost every line of human endeavor. This is a great reconstruction period. It is rich with opportunity for professional salespeople who have the imagination to build their efforts around motives that are beneficial to the general public and who release their full energies through their work.

Racial privileges are passing. Mass privileges are in the ascendancy. Remember this too when selecting a motive as a guiding spirit of your sales efforts: the people must be served. The whole of America stands at the crossroads of progress, waiting for able leadership. Millions of people have been slowed down by fear and indecision. Here is an unparalleled opportunity for men and women who are prepared to adapt themselves to the new brand of leadership, fortified by courage dedicated to service.

High-pressure salesmanship, of which we heard so much during the recent decades, is now a thing of the past. The go-getter will have to make room for the go-giver in every walk of life, selling included. Successful leaders of the future, whether in the field of selling or in other walks of life, must make the Golden Rule the basis for their leadership. In the future the question of paramount importance will be, how much can I give in the way of service to others? rather than how much can I get away with and keep out of jail?

A great economic renaissance is sweeping the entire world. Anyone who cannot see this is mentally and morally blind. The old order of things and business in industry has already been swept away, and the new order is rapidly taking its place. Wise beyond description are those who see this change and adapt themselves to it harmoniously, without force. We are approaching an era during which we shall see the reincarnation of the spirit of Thomas Jefferson, Benjamin Franklin, George Washington, and Abraham Lincoln in politics, and the reincarnation of the spirit of Marshall Field and John Wanamaker in industry, business, and finance.

People have become rebellious against the oppression forced upon them by the avaricious and the greedy. This spirit of resentment is not transient; it will remain until it rights a wrong. It will gain organized momentum. America will not soon again see the sad spectacle of millions of people starving to death in the midst of an overabundance of both the necessities and the luxuries of life. We are on the grand concourse that leads out of the wilderness of human exploitation, and we are not going to be driven or coerced into giving up our rights to remain on this highway.

In recent years, we in the United States have been losing our ability to compete. For a long time, we could pay the world's highest wages with no problems. We were ahead of the parade in inventions and in productivity per man-hour. We had huge natural resources and didn't need to import much, so we had the best of all possible worlds: both self-sufficiency and competitiveness.

That's why from 1896 until the 1970s, Uncle Sam invariably had trade surpluses. What has happened to us?

We have received a double whammy. First, because of our high living standards, we have run through much of our natural treasure house. The Mesabi Hematites in Minnesota, which produced iron ores, have pooped out, and we had to go to Ongaba in southwestern Africa and the Orinoco in Venezuela for iron ores. Our copper no longer sufficed, and we had to turn to Chile and the Congo. We have come increasingly to depend on Canada, Venezuela, and the Middle East for oil. To buy these commodities, we need foreign exchange, which requires either dribbling away our diminishing gold reserves or selling American gold abroad. Second, other nations have bright, energetic, and skillful people who have learned our mass-production tricks. We have seen a constant loss of American jobs.

America has turned the corner. We're going to have to get to work. We can't hide behind new tariff walls, not as long as we must buy more and more foreign raw materials. We must modernize. We must produce not only more per man-hour, but more per wage dollar.

These statements of fact, and of prophecy, may be helpful to those who aspire to leadership in selling or in some other walk of life. Those who have imagination will not wait for time to prove their soundness. They will anticipate the changes that are to take place and will adapt themselves to the new conditions. The great changes occasioned by economic upheavals, which have thrown millions out of adjustment in all fields of human activity, accentuate the need for discovering those fundamental principles by which one may come back into the path of ordered progress.

Since all people must use some form of salesmanship to promote themselves and adjust themselves to satisfactory relations, both social and commercial, it behooves one to lend an ear to a presentation of those fundamental principles with suggestions for their practical application. This book attempts to teach such principles. Those who master these fundamental principles of persuasion can sell their way through life, successfully surmounting obstacles, overcoming opposition, and harnessing and redirecting adverse forces.

No matter who you are or how much you know, you will not succeed unless you are a salesperson. You must sell your services, you must sell your knowledge, you must sell yourself, you must sell your personality. As you approach the study of fundamentals, keep ever before you the fact that your only limitations are creatures of your own mind. Remember too that you can remove any limitation you create. This book was written for men and women who will not permit themselves to be bound down by blind circumstance or hedged in by psychological limitations.

Chapter Two

YOU NEED INTELLIGENT
PROMOTION TO SUCCEED

It may be true that the world will beat a path to your door if you make a better mousetrap than your neighbor, even though your house may be far back in the woods, but you may as well know that the big rush toward your place of business will not begin until you have given the location and have properly promoted your product.

Jack Dempsey was a good but unknown prizefighter. He stepped up front and won the world championship, with its million-dollar income, only after boxing manager Jack Kearns had promoted him into that highly desirable position. Jack Dempsey's fists and arms did the punching, but Jack Kearns' brain guided the blows so they would find their way into big bank balances. Kearns' promotion of Dempsey was so effective that even long after he lost the championship, Dempsey was still able to collect big dividends from the mere use of his name.

Thomas A. Edison, with less than three months of schooling, became the world's greatest inventor because he possessed that rare quality of being able to promote himself. Where he succeeded, no fewer than ten thousand other inventors, many of them as capable as he, never have been heard of and never will be.

Jimmy Starr was a run-of-the-mill newspaperman, no better and no worse than a thousand others in his profession, until William Randolph Hearst spread his name on the front page of all his newspapers; then Starr became America's leading columnist. There were others who could write better material than Starr ever wrote, but you would not recognize one of them, because they had not been properly promoted.

During the First World War, Napoleon Hill's attention was called to a man by the name of Arthur Nash, a Cincinnati merchant tailor who had taken his employees into business with him and had given them a part of the profits, because his business was on the rocks and he saw no other way of saving it from bankruptcy. Hill went to Cincinnati, interviewed Nash, and wrote the first story about him. In his story he called him "Golden Rule Nash."

The story was picked up by newspapers and magazines all over the country, and Nash received free publicity for more than five years. When the merchant died a dozen years later, he was a wealthy man, and his business was among the most successful of its time.

Rudolph Valentino was dancing up and down Broadway at a few dollars per dance when a film director discovered him and gave him a clever promoter. Valentino soon became one of the biggest silent movie stars and the screen's greatest lover; the women of America ate it up.

When the talkies came in the late 1920s, most of the stars of the silent era had to be replaced overnight, because they had no real ability for speaking roles. The great lovers of the silents were great only because they had been cleverly promoted as such; the talkies proved that.

Impresario Florenz Ziegfeld picked up humorist Will Rogers when he was an unknown gum-chewing, rope-throwing vaudeville specialist—when he could get an engagement. With proper promotions, Ziegfeld catapulted Rogers into stardom almost overnight, to say nothing of paving the way for motion picture and other money-making opportunities from which Rogers made millions. Before Ziegfeld's promotion caught up with him, Rogers was glad to appear before clubs for his lunch in cities where he was playing on the vaudeville stage.

This same promoter took over Eddie "Banjo Eyes" Cantor and started him on a career that paid him $10,000 a week for merely reading lines that someone else wrote. Ziegfeld also promoted the tall, slender comedienne Fanny Brice into the big money. Not one of these all-time greats would have piled up their huge fortunes if it had not been for clever promotion.

More recently, we have had Johnny Cash. He was a competent singer with a modicum of success when his wife, June Carter, took him in charge and began to promote him. He went on to become one of the greatest country music stars of all time. Moreover, he made himself wealthy. He had just as much talent then as he had before, but now he became better paid.

When Hill was organizing the law of success philosophy, Andrew Carnegie sent him to call on Henry Ford. "You want to watch this man Ford," said Carnegie, "for one day he is going to dominate the motor industry of America." Hill went to Detroit and met Ford for the first time in 1908. When he first looked him over, Hill wondered how Andrew Carnegie, as shrewd a judge of character as he was, could have been so mistaken in his estimation of Ford, but year by year, Ford climbed to the top of his field. Behind his stupendous achievement there was a highly organized, systematic and effective promotion. Perhaps no man did a greater service to him than W. J. Cameron, the chief Ford promoter, who saw to it that the Ford interests were never neglected in the eyes of the public. During that time, no less than a hundred other makers of automobiles rose and fell like mushrooms because they did not have the foresight to surround themselves with promotion experts.

By promotion experts, we do not mean advertising people. Promotion is one thing; advertising is something entirely different. Promotion is the art of keeping an individual favorably sold to the public all the time. The late Ivy Lee was one of the greatest promotion men of his time. It was he who removed the stigma from the name of John D. Rockefeller Sr. and kept his name before the public and in a favorable light almost continuously. Ivy Lee seldom worked through paid publicity. He preferred free space and other, more efficient forms of promotion for keeping his clients properly sold to the public.

While Napoleon Hill was publishing *Golden Rule Magazine*, he wrote a brief editorial praising the work of John D. Rockefeller Jr. in connection with his fine humanitarian work in going to Colorado to settle the famous coal strike of 1919. Almost before the print had dried on the article, Hill received a wire from Ivy Lee inviting him to visit him in New York. When Hill met him, Lee got down to business without ceremonies, offering Hill $10,000 a year (around $120,000 in 2020 dollars) to join his staff and write similar editorials about other clients of his. Promotion experts earn and receive big money because they have the ability to recognize, and the good sense to appropriate, the forces needed to further the interests of their clients. Hill declined Ivy Lee's offer, but he often regretted the mistake after coming to realize that a few years of schooling under that genius could have been worth many times the sum he had been offered.

Few readers have probably ever heard of America's greatest thinker, Stuart Austin Wier, who lived in Dallas, Texas, where he practiced law. There may be no living person today who has the depth and balance of thought that Mr. Wier possessed, and very likely no philosopher from Socrates to Elbert Hubbard ever possessed his flexibility of thought, variety of knowledge, and balance of judgment. But Wier is practically unknown because he did not choose to avail himself of professional promotion services.

One who did was Alvin York, an illiterate Tennessee mountaineer who objected to conscription during World War I. He put up such a howl about his conscientious objection that he attracted much attention and plenty of newspaper space. But he finally entered the Army and became one of the war's most decorated soldiers.

After York's return from war, he was still illiterate, but a clever promoter took him over. In 1926, a large high school in Jamestown, Tennessee, was opened with his name. The state of Tennessee dedicated one of its main highways to him, and he received financial and other forms of aid from influential people all over the country.

When Theodore Roosevelt came back from Africa just after he left the White House in 1909, he made his first public appearance at New York's Madison Square Garden. Before he would agree to make the appearance, he carefully arranged for nearly a thousand paid applauders to be scattered throughout the audience to applaud his entrance on the platform. For more than fifteen minutes, these paid hand clappers made the place ring with their enthusiasm. The other sheep took up the suggestion and joined in for another quarter hour. The newspapermen present were swept off their feet by the tremendous ovation given the American hero, and his name was emblazoned across the headlines of the newspapers in letters two inches high. Teddy understood and made intelligent use of personal promotion. That was the major reason why he was a great statesman.

Conversely, one does not have to be an expert on propaganda or personal promotion tactics to observe how effectively these forces were used by Mussolini, Hitler, and Stalin, and later by Castro and Mao Zedong.

Down through the ages, men like these have sought to keep themselves constantly promoted in all sorts of favorable lights to appease home folks and impress foreigners. Even a street can be made to take on a different reputation and yield greater rents under the right sort of promotional direction. New York's Fifth Avenue is known the world over as the street of elegant shops. This reputation enables owners to ask for and receive fabulous rentals for their property. Fifth Avenue's reputation is maintained by the Fifth Avenue Association through a carefully managed plan that keeps out riffraff.

Truly, it pays to be properly promoted. Elvis Presley was one entertainer who skyrocketed to stardom. He had a pleasing voice and a rather undefined character, but he also had Colonel Tom Parker. As a result of Parker's astute management, Presley was able to demand and receive astronomical fees for his personal appearances, records, and movies.

When she lived in the White House, Mrs. John F. Kennedy was not known merely as the president's wife; she was known for herself. Professional promotion experts saw to that. Whether or not this exploitation of Mrs. Kennedy as an individual separate and distinct from the president was in good taste, she was neither idle nor without income from her independent sources of service.

One might think that a person as prominent as the wife of the president of the United States would not need professional promotion, but Mrs. Kennedy was keen enough to realize that no one is so big or so important that he or she cannot be raised higher through well-organized promotion.

How do these ideas apply in your case? One of the major duties of life is selling one's way to some definite goal. Not all of us are efficient salespeople. Therefore most of us need the services of experienced promotion experts who will assume the responsibility of keeping us steadily and favorably before the public.

In 1905 an enterprising young lawyer in Chicago by the name of Paul Harris conceived the brilliant idea of circumventing rules against lawyers advertising themselves. He gathered around him thirty or so of his business friends and organized the first Rotary Club, the idea being, of course, to promote himself among a variety of contacts, which might conceivably be converted into clients as a result of his personal contact with them once a week.

Today the Rotary Club movement has spread all over the world and has become an international power for good. The movement did its founder no harm. Doctors, dentists, lawyers, architects, and others whose professional ethics prohibited direct advertising of themselves profited by Paul Harris's example.

Ethics is one thing, building up a professional practice is another, and the two can be made to harmonize. That is the business of promotion experts, and that goes for the rest of us as well. If we wish to get ahead in the world, we must find ways and means of bringing ourselves to the attention of people who need whatever we have to offer the world. Building a better mousetrap than one's neighbor will avail one nothing unless sound, intense, and continuous sales promotion is placed back of the trap.

Actors walk hungrily up and down Broadway trying to sell themselves. Once in a blue moon a Ziegfeld discovers an Eddie Cantor or a Will Rogers or a Fanny Brice and promotes him or her to the top, but blue moons do not come often. The better plan is not to wait for discovery, no matter who you are or what you have to offer the world. It is to search until you find the one person best equipped to market the sort of services you have to offer. Then give that person a good block of stock in yourself and tell him or her to go ahead and promote you.

A young man acknowledged as one of the coming musical composers and pianists once visited Napoleon Hill. He spent two hours trying to convince Hill that there was virtue in the old habit of an artist starving in an attic rather than commercializing his art. The young visitor tried conscientiously to convince Hill that the philosophy of opulence, as outlined in his book *Think and Grow Rich*, was an insult to great artists, whose major business, from this man's viewpoint, should be a willingness to starve for their art. The musician had a pleasing personality, a brilliant mind, and a great passion for classical music, but it was obvious that his warped view of life would cost him his much coveted goal: to be recognized as a great musician. He was already a great artist, but the world did not know him. Unless he allied himself with a set of brains skilled at marketing his services, he would go through life an unknown genius. The irony of this story is that this genius came to Hill's apartment to pick up a cast-off suit and an overcoat he had been promised.

The editor of a syndicated service once stated that every well-known man in the literary field reaches the top through clever promotion. He mentioned in particular the late Dr. Frank Crane, who wrote a daily newspaper column in a light vein. "When Dr. Crane first came to us," said this distinguished editor, "he was peddling his stuff here and there, wherever he could get a country weekly newspaper to buy it, not earning enough to keep him and his family." When Dr. Crane died, he was making upwards of $75,000 annually, all of it from the sale of that same column, marketed by an expert promotion man.

Elbert Hubbard made a sizable fortune by writing and marketing his own works, but the world seldom knows more than one Elbert Hubbard at a time. He was one of those very rare persons with the ability to create and market the products of their creation. Most of us are lucky if we have the ability to create, much less sell, our products.

Napoleon Hill spent a quarter of a century organizing the philosophy of individual achievement. He wrote into that philosophy all that had been retrieved from the experiences of such men as Andrew Carnegie, Henry Ford, Thomas A. Edison, John Wanamaker, and others of their type. Yet he found himself outstripped in financial income by men who wrote books they had thrown together overnight. Hill finally awakened to the fact, and placed himself under the management of W. Clement Stone. More was accomplished in the way of recognition during the first year of Mr. Stone's management than had been accomplished during all the previous years, when Hill served as his own manager.

It is each person's duty and responsibility to provide himself with whatever form of promotion is needed to help him attain success in his chosen calling. R. Lee Sharpe expressed this thought beautifully in his poem "Princes and Kings."

Isn't it strange how princes and kings,
and clowns that caper in sawdust rings,
and common people, like you and me,
are builders for eternity?

Each is given a list of rules;
a shapeless mass; a bag of tools.
And each must fashion, ere life is flown,
A stumbling block, or a Stepping-Stone.

Self-advancement cannot be built on bluff, fear, or flattery. Success in life demands sterner stuff than these. Mere words and fine platitudes will never take the place of a practical plan doggedly put into action. And this despite the fact that a book which has sold millions of copies admonishes the reader to flatter those whom he wishes to sway and attract. A book on flattery may be helpful to those willing to stoop to it. But what about those unfortunates on whom the purchasers of the book will work their magic? Are they to be deprived of protection against these seductive flatterers?

If we used flattery in our work, we would be instantly pegged as charlatans, and rightfully so. We get better results by frankness in our dealings with people, for we find that direct, straight dealing not only wins friends but also holds them.

Morons and nitwits like to be flattered. There is no denying this fact, but people who make any real pretense of thinking resent all forms of flattery; it is an insult to their intelligence. When anyone starts to flatter you, it is a sure indication that that person wants something you possess or some favor from you. Flattery is a form of dope, which sidetracks the reasoning faculty of the one flattered. While it may and often does permit the flatterer to gain temporary advantages, the time comes when the effect wears off and the victim comes out from under the spell with resentment.

The most that can be said of flattery is that it is a cheap psychological trick with which charlatans and dishonest people lull others into a state of carelessness while they pick their pockets. Flattery is the chief tool of all confidence men. Through its use, crooked stockbrokers take millions of dollars away from men and women annually. Through its use, vicious spies inveigle their way into the confidence of military men and wheedle information out of them. Mercenary women use flattery as a weapon with which to break down the resistance of men who will not respond to mere sex appeal.

One highly publicized showgirl who was married many times managed to pick a millionaire every time she married, because she was adept at the art of flattery, but the marriages did not last. Nothing built on flattery can last, for flattery as a weapon for ensnaring people is designed and executed by the devil. Those who permit themselves to be influenced by flattery are whipped before the battle begins. Marilyn Monroe's downfall really began when she started to pay more attention to the flattery of producers and wealthy men than she gave to her business.

Some executives demand a flock of yes-men around them; they would be safer if they employed a staff of no-men. The human ego is a tricky piece of mental equipment. It needs constant protection against all forms of flattery, the one element to which the ego responds most readily. One of the commonest mistakes is seeking the counsel of friends, because most so-called friends would rather flatter than be frank; they do not wish to offend. Therefore their opinions are usually worthless and misleading. Film stars and other quick money victims shine for a time and then flicker out mainly because they blow up and burst by feeding too freely on public flattery.

It is said that John W. Davis, a lawyer who was the Democratic presidential candidate in 1924. was paid an enormous sum annually by the J. P. Morgan banking firm, not for what he told the members of the firm they *could* do but for what he told them they could *not* do. He was the official no-man of the firm. There was no flattering to win and influence. The Morgan partners, astute businessmen that they were, preferred cold facts to flattery.

Al Smith, the Democratic presidential candidate in 1928, climbed from the fish market to within a stone's throw of the White House. His greatest help was Mrs. Belle Moskowitz, his official no-woman.

Truly great business leaders do not depend upon flattery to get results. They have a better formula. Andrew Carnegie did not flatter Charles M. Schwab. He got more dependable results by paying Mr. Schwab as much as a million dollars a year for his brains and his personality, demanding loyalty and getting it.

The train dispatcher does not flatter the conductor; he gives the conductor definite orders which he does not question. Once in a while the orders may be neglected; then a wreck costs the conductor his job or his life.

There are times when one should say yes and times when one should say no. The author of a best seller, who advised her readers as one of twelve disciplines to say yes to all questions asked for one whole day, could have been deeply embarrassed had she literally followed her own counsel. Life is made up of situations and circumstances calling for yesses and noes. The person who negotiates his way through life successfully learns to use each in its proper place. Lincoln kept bitter enemies as members of his cabinet because he needed their frank analysis and criticism. Woodrow Wilson ousted cabinet members who did not agree with him. The difference in the records of the two presidents is very great.

How far will a military man get in warfare if soldiers are managed by flattery? If you haven't seen the film *Patton*, please do. You will also see why George C. Scott, who won the Academy Award for Best Actor for his role in the film, turned down the award: because he did not need the flattery of an Oscar.

Flattery would not help one very much with most policemen and taxicab drivers. Those who make themselves indispensable to others by rendering more and better service than they are paid to render will accomplish more permanent and desirable results than they could accomplish with all the flattery in the world.

If you would sell your way through life successfully, look around you and see what useful service you can render to as many people as possible. Make yourself of value to others, and you will not need to learn the art of flattery in order to win people and use personal influence. Moreover, those you do win will stay won. To be well liked gives one great advantage, but flattery is not the tool with which this desirable end may be attained and held.

A pleasing personality is worth a king's ransom to those who possess it, but such a personality is not developed through speaking words of flattery, which mean nothing. A pleasing personality consists of thirty different characteristics, which can be developed. You will find the complete description of these thirty assets in the original edition of *Think and Grow Rich*. Master them and make them your own property; then you will be able to attract and hold friends. There are practical and tried rules for attracting and holding friends. They are the rules gleaned from the life work of Abraham Lincoln, Benjamin Franklin, Thomas Paine, Thomas Jefferson, Samuel Adams, Richard Henry Lee, George Washington, and half a hundred other truly great men who laid the foundation of this country. They are also the rules used by the most successful business and industrial leaders the country has produced: Andrew Carnegie, Thomas Edison, Henry Ford, John Wanamaker, F. W. Woolworth, H. Ross Perot, and W. Clement Stone. If any one of these men had advocated flattery as a means of getting ahead in the world, their recommendation would have been impressive, but not one of them used or recommended so low and vulgar method as a means of self-advancement. When flattery and direct frankness are placed side by side, the latter will win over the former nine hundred and ninety nine times out of every thousand.

F. Lee Bailey said, "Every truly great trial lawyer knows that attempts to flatter a jury are always fraught with definite hazards to his case." The most successful lawyers are those who deal with facts instead of relying upon flattery. The same is true of successful business executives. How far, for example, do you believe one would have gotten by trying to influence Howard Hughes through flattery?

If we appear to be overemphasizing the importance of the dangers of relying upon flattery as a means of selling one's way through life, it is because of the possible effects upon the large number of people, who have been taught to use flattery as the hub of the wheel of personal advancement. This philosophy is dangerous to all who embrace it; it is especially hazardous to the young person just starting out with little or no experience in the business world.

There are sound and commendable ways of winning friends and influencing people through appeals based upon some combination of the nine basic motives, described in chapter 4. If you wish to climb to the top of the ladder of success and remain there, it will be much safer to use these nine motives as the rungs of your ladder instead of depending upon flattery. Every move, every act, and every fault of every human being of sound body and mind who has reached the age of reason is influenced by one or more of the nine basic motives.

When you come to the description of these motives, study it carefully. Learn how to influence people by genuine appeal to natural motives; then you will experience no resentment from those whom you influence. Success in any calling is largely a matter of being able to negotiate one's way through life with a minimum amount of friction in relationships with other people. By mastering, understanding, and applying the nine basic motives, you may reduce misunderstandings, opposition, and friction to a minimum. Do this and you will be a great salesman, no matter what you are selling.

Lest all this counsel impress you as mere preachment, let Napoleon Hill tell you how he made practical use of his own philosophy of personal negotiation:

At the end of the first year of the Depression, I found myself divested of my money and most of my worldly property. People were not interested in books; they were interested in eating. I closed my New York office and moved to Washington, D.C., where I planned to remain until the economic storm had passed.

Months stretched into years, and instead of the Depression passing, it became worse. Finally I reached a decision not to wait for the end of the business stagnation, but to go on the lecture platform and work my way back into useful service to others who also had been wounded.

I decided to make my start in Washington. For this purpose, I needed newspaper space for advertising. The amount of space I required would cost over $2,000, and I did not have this amount, neither could I get it from the usual banking sources.

Here I was face-to-face with a situation similar to that which you and every other person on earth must sometime experience: I was a need of something I had to procure with mere words. Here then is a brief description of exactly what I did and said in order to surmount my problem. I went to Colonel Leroy Heron, advertising director of *The Washington Star*, and made known to him my needs, and approaching him, I had two courses available to me. I could flatter him. I could tell him what a great paper he represented, what a fine record he made in the World War, what a great advertising man I believed him to be, and all that sort of piffle. Or I could lay all my cards on the table and tell him what I wanted, why I wanted it, and why I believed I should get it. I chose the latter method of approach.

Then I was forced to decide whether I would disclose to Colonel Heron all the facts, including my financial weakness, or skip over these embarrassing subjects without clearly discussing them. Again, I chose to rely upon frankness and directness. There come times in one's life when no other plan will secure the desired results. As well as I can remember, I told him, "Colonel Heron, I wish to use *The Washington Star* and an advertising campaign to announce a series of public lectures on the philosophy of individual achievement. The space I require will amount to approximately $2,500.

"My problem is in the unpleasant fact that I do not have that amount of money available. I had that amount and more a short time ago, but the Depression consumed it. My request for this credit is not based upon the usual commercial credit rating. On that basis, I would not be entitled to the credit. My appeal is based upon the fact, plenty of evidence of which I am prepared to present to you here and now, that I have devoted a quarter of a century to the study of the principles of individual achievement. During this time, I have had the active cooperation of such men as Andrew Carnegie, Thomas A. Edison, Frank A. Vanderlip, John Wanamaker, and Cyrus H. K. Curtis. These men thought enough of me to give freely of their time and experience over a long period of years while I was organizing the Philosophy of Success. The time each gave to me was worth many times the amount of credit I am asking of you. Through their cooperation, I'm now prepared to take to the world a philosophy of self-help which all the people of the world badly need. If you do not wish to extend to me the credit as a sound business risk, then extend it in the same spirit of helpfulness that these men of affairs gave to me of their time and experience."

The credit was extended to me by Colonel Heron on my brief statement of my case with this significant remark: "I do not know what are your chances of paying for the space you want, but I believe I know enough of human nature to understand that you intend to pay for the space. I also believe that any philosophy organized from the life work of such men as Edison and Carnegie is sound and needed at this time. Moreover, I believe anyone to whom these men would devote their priceless time is worthy of much more credit than you seek with the *Star*. Bring in your copy, and I will run it. We will talk to the credit manager afterward."

After the transaction had been completed and the advertising had been paid for, I called on Colonel Heron again and had a very intimate personal talk with him. I asked him to tell me frankly why he extended the credit in face of the fact that I told him all about my financial weakness and nothing whatsoever of my ability to pay the account. His reply was illuminating: "I gave you the credit," he explained, "because you made no attempt to cover up your financial weakness. You resorted to no subterfuge and did not set your best foot forward first."

How far do you suppose I would have gotten had I appealed to Colonel Heron on anything but frankness?

The old-time salesman carried with him a supply of cigars, good liquor, and burlesque stories with which to entertain his prospective buyers. All of these have been supplanted by films and highly colored graphs and charts with which the salesperson can paint a perfect picture of the merchandise in the mind of the prospective buyer.

There are nine windows and doors through which the human mind can be entered and influenced. Not one of these is labeled "flattery." The nine doors are the nine basic motives by which all people are influenced.

Remember, as you read and absorb the contents of this book, that it is not a book on flattery. It is not a course on pleasantries and platitudes. It is not a course on psychological tricks and legerdemain. It is a course based on the recorded facts and realities of life as they have been organized from experiences of the most able leaders the country has ever produced. Seek the counsel of men who will tell you the truth about yourself even if it hurts you to hear it. Mere commendation will not bring the improvement you need.

Chapter Three

THE STRATEGY OF
PROFESSIONAL SALESMANSHIP

Motive is the seed from which a sale may be germinated. All seeds must contain the life germ, or they will not germinate, regardless of the soil in which they are planted. Motive too must contain the life germ, or it will not germinate into a sale.

Those who understand how to inject the germ of life into motive are professional salespeople. They are professionals because they capture the prospective buyer's own imagination and make it work for them. When an appropriate motive has been painted in the mind of the prospective buyer by a real artist, it begins to work from within as yeast works on bread dough.

Let us illustrate this point. The late Dr. William Rainey Harper, while serving as president of the Uni-

versity of Chicago, desired to construct a new building on the campus, the estimated cost of which was
$1 million. His available funds were not sufficient for
his needs; nor did he see any chance of securing the
necessary funds from the university's annual budget.
After analysis of the situation, it became apparent to
Dr. Harper that he would have to seek $1 million from
an outside source.

Here begins the description of the modus operandi
of a professional salesperson. Dr. Harper did not start
buttonholing wealthy men for donations; he did not put
on a drive for donations. He made up his mind to get the
entire sum through a single sale. Moreover, he personally
assumed the responsibility for making the sale.

His first move was to lay out a plan of action. Here all
except professional salespeople usually fall down: for lack
of a plan that is both definite and sound. His plan, when
completed, involved only two prospective donors. From
one or the other, he intended to secure the needed funds.
His plan was conceived with ingenuity and rounded out
with a keen, penetrating strategy that was loaded with
dynamite.

What did Dr. Harper do? He chose as his prospective donors two Chicago millionaires whom he knew to
be bitter enemies. You are no doubt beginning to see the
point before it has been explained, but follow on and get
the technique of a professional sales artist.

One of these men was the head of the Chicago street railway system. The other was a politician who had accumulated a great fortune by gouging the streetcar company and other methods. Dr. Harper's selection of prospective buyers for his plan was perfect. Here again is a point at which all but professional artists at selling are usually weak: they do not use sound judgment in the selection of prospective buyers.

After turning his plan over in his mind for a few days and carefully rehearsing his sales presentation, Dr. Harper swung into action. Choosing the noon hour as the most favorable for his call, he presented himself at the office of the streetcar magnate. Observe with profit his reason for choosing this particular hour: he deduced that the executive's secretary would be at lunch at that hour and that his prospect would be alone in his office.

His deduction proved correct. Finding the outer office empty, he walked on into the private office. The magnate looked up at the intruder in surprise and asked, "What can I do for you, sir?"

"I beg your pardon for the intrusion," Dr. Harper replied. "I am Dr. Harper, president of the University of Chicago. I found no one in the outer office, so I took the liberty of walking in."

"Well, yes, of course," the other exclaimed, "Have a seat, Dr. Harper. I'm glad to have the honor of a visit."

"Thank you," the doctor replied. "I'm in a great hurry and will stand, if you don't mind. I just dropped in to tell you of an idea that has been running in my mind for some time."

Here comes the motive; watch how deftly it is planted in fertile soil. "First of all, I want to tell you how greatly I admire the wonderful system of street railway transportation you have given the people of Chicago." Neutralizing his prospect's mind.

"I believe it to be the greatest system in the country. It has occurred to me, however, that while you have built a great monument to your name, it is of such a nature that the world will forget who built it the moment you die." Watch the professional go back now to motive. "I would like to see you build a monument that will endure forever. I've thought of a plan by which you might build such a monument, but I've met with some difficulties, which I'm sorry to say may stand in the way," pulling the lure away from the prospect to make the idea more desirable. "I had thought of securing for you the privilege of constructing a beautiful granite building on the university campus, but some of the members of our board want this privilege to go to Mr. X," Dr. Harper said, mentioning the name of the political enemy. "I'm holding out in your favor and just came by to ask if you can think of any plan that may help me to secure this rare privilege for you."

"That is most interesting," the magnate exclaimed. "Please sit down and let us talk about the matter."

"I'm exceedingly sorry," Dr. Harper replied, "But we are having a board meeting in an hour, and I must hurry along. If you think of an argument I might use in your behalf, please telephone me as promptly as possible, and I'll go to bat for you before the board. Good day, sir."

Dr. Harper turned and walked out. When he reached his office, he found that the streetcar magnate had already telephoned him three times requesting that Dr. Harper call him as soon as he came in. The educator was obliging. He telephoned the magnate, who requested that he be permitted to come out and present his case to the board in person. Dr. Harper replied that this would be inadvisable, that in view of the opposition some of the board members had expressed toward him, Dr. Harper might present the matter more diplomatically (intensifying the allure). "If you will telephone me tomorrow morning," Dr. Harper suggested, "I will let you know about luck I've had."

The next morning, upon arriving at his office, Dr. Harper found the streetcar magnate already there. They were closeted together for half an hour. What happened probably will never be known to the public. The interesting thing, however, is that the streetcar magnate assumed the role of salesman, while Dr. Harper became the buyer and was persuaded to accept a check for a million dollars and promise that he would try to get it accepted by the board.

The check was accepted. What arguments Dr. Harper used with the board no one knows, but the million-dollar building now stands on the campus of the university—silent but impressive evidence that mastery and selling are never accidental. The building bears the name of the donor.

Hearing of this incident, Napoleon Hill called on Dr. Harper and asked him to explain why some of the members of his board should prefer to honor a racketeering politician. In reply he merely shrugged his shoulders and smiled, a queer little twinkle in his eyes. His answer was sufficient. The opposition existed mainly in Dr. Harper's imagination. To place the transaction in the category of justified strategy, Dr. Harper probably developed the idea of friendly opposition in the minds of some of the members of his board.

Let us analyze this transaction to make sure that the fine points are not overlooked. First of all, observe that no high-pressure methods were used by Dr. Harper. He depended entirely upon motive to turn the tide for him. No doubt he spent days planning his approach. Incidentally, the motive he chose is one of the most alluring of all. In fact, he made his appeal through two motives, namely (a) desire for fame and power, and (b) revenge. The streetcar magnate saw instantly that he could perpetuate his name as a public benefactor in such a way that it would go marching on long after his remains had gone back to dust and his street railway system had perhaps been supplanted by some other mode of travel. Also, thanks to Dr. Harper's sound strategy, he saw an opportunity to get revenge on his bitterest enemy by depriving him of a great honor.

No great amount of imagination is required to see what would have happened if Dr. Harper had made his approach in the usual manner by writing a letter to the streetcar magnate asking for an appointment, thus giving him an opportunity to anticipate the motive behind the request. Any but a professional salesman would have made the approach either in this way or by presenting himself at the man's office and requesting him to help the university out of a hole by giving it a million dollars.

Suppose for illustration that Dr. Harper had not understood the psychology of motive and had not been a professional salesman. He would have visited the magnate, and this is something like the conversation that would have taken place:

"Good morning, sir. I'm Dr. Harper, president of the University of Chicago. I've come to ask for a few minutes of your time," asking for favors to begin with instead of offering favors and failing to neutralize the prospective buyer's mind. "We need an extra million dollars for a new building, which we intend to erect on the campus of the university, and I thought you might be interested in donating the amount. You've been successful. You have a great street railway system, from which you earn big profits, profits which really have been made possible through the patronage of the public. Now it is only fair that you should show your appreciation of the success which the public has made possible for you by doing something for the public good."

Observe this scene in your mind's eye. The streetcar magnate is fidgeting in his chair and nervously fussing with some papers on his desk, groping for an alibi with which to refuse. As soon as the university president hesitates for a moment in his sales presentation, the magnate takes up the conversation. "I'm exceedingly sorry, Dr. Harper, but our budget for philanthropic purposes has been entirely exhausted. You know, we make a liberal annual donation to the Community Chest fund. There is nothing more we can do this year. Besides, a million dollars is a large sum of money. I'm sure our board could not be persuaded to donate so much money to charity." He beats the doctor to that word *charity*.

You see, of course, that a poor presentation would have placed Dr. Harper in the unhappy position of one who begs for charity. Giving to charity as such is not listed as one of the nine basic motives which move people to action. But lift the word *charity* out of its humble setting and give it the color of privilege, fame, and honor, and it takes on an entirely different meaning. Only a professional salesperson can do this.

One way is clever; the other is crude. The act of selling, if scientifically conducted, may be compared to an artist who, stroke by stroke, develops form and harmony and blends the colors on a canvas. Professional salespeople paint word pictures of the things they are offering for sale. The canvas on which they paint is the imagination of the prospective buyer. They first roughly outline the picture they want to paint, later filling in the details, using ideas for paint. In the center of the picture, at the focal point, they draw a clearly defined outline of motive. Just as a painting on a canvas must be based upon a motif or a theme, so must a successful sale.

The picture the professional sales artist paints in the mind of the prospective buyer must be more than a mere skeleton outline. Details must be perfected so the prospect not only sees the picture in perspective as a finished whole, but as a pleasing one. Motive is what determines how pleasing the picture is.

The amateur is like a little child, who may draw a rough picture of a horse that can be vaguely recognized. When the professional artist draws a picture of a horse, those who see it not only recognize it as a horse but exclaim, "How wonderful! How like a living thing." The artist paints action, reality, and life into the picture.

There is the same difference between those who call themselves salespeople and the professional salesperson as there is between the dabbler and the master painter. Inefficient salespeople hurriedly sketch a crude outline of the thing they wish to sell, leaving motive out of the picture. They say, "See, there it is, as plain as the nose on your face. Now will you buy?" But prospective buyers do not see what the salesman has in his or her own mind, or they may see but do not feel. They are not moved to action by any rough sketch or unfinished, lifeless picture. No seed of desire has been planted in their minds, no appeal to motive. That's why poor salespeople don't get the results desired.

Professional salespeople paint a different kind of picture. They omit no detail. They mix their word colorings so that they blend with harmony and symmetry to capture the prospective buyer's imagination. They build the picture around a motive that dominates the entire scene, putting the prospect's own mind to work on their behalf. That is professional salesmanship.

As everyone knows, life insurance is abstract, intangible, and one of the hardest things in the world to sell. One cannot see it; one cannot smell it or taste it or feel it or sense it through any of the five senses. In addition to these handicaps, one must die in order to profit by it. Even then the profit goes to someone else. No amateur is a successful life insurance salesperson.

By contrast, professionals familiarize themselves with the motives that quickly and effectively appeal to the prospective purchaser of life insurance. They analyze prospective buyers accurately in order to readily catalogue them as to the motive best suited for each case. They will place before the prospect's eyes an invisible canvas, and on this canvas, with only words for brushes and paints, draw a picture of the prospect twenty years in the future, aged and infirm. They can play on the prospect's heart-strings as a professional violinist plays on the strings of a Stradivarius.

Or the professional could go further. They might add another scene, portraying the client as cold and dead. Beside the casket is a helpless and dependent old spouse— the person the prospect loves and wishes to make secure. The picture can be so realistic as to be haunting. By planting in it the motives of fear and love, the salesperson makes a friendly ally of the prospect's own mind.

Only an artist can paint such a picture, yet artists are made, not born. Someone may be born with inherent talent, but will become a finished artist only by mastering the technique of harmony, form, and color. Sales artists too are made and not born. They become masters by studying technique and motive. They develop expert methods of analyzing buyers and the things they buy. Dr. Harper was not a born salesman; he was small in physique and unprepossessing in appearance. He became a great salesman by studying people and the motives that cause them to act.

That is exactly what all who would attain mastery in selling must do. The old bromide about salespeople being born and not made is as weak as it is old. The one hundred thousand salespeople we have trained have taught us that salespeople can be made. As educators of salespeople, we have had the privilege of knowing intimately perhaps as many as a hundred genuinely professional salespeople. Most of the others in the sales field whom we have known, numbering well into the thousands, have been just plain order takers.

The difference in earning capacity between a professional salesperson and an order taker is very great. It runs all the way from several thousand dollars to as much as a million dollars a year. The late industrialist John W. Gates earned $1 million a year with much less effort than most salespeople earned $3,000. He was an artist. The late Diamond Jim Brady had no difficulty in converting his talents into a like amount of money. Brady too was a professional. These two men, and all others in their class, used showmanship, technique, and method, whereas most salespeople depend upon shoe leather instead of technique and method.

Professional salesmanship consists of a series of picture impressions that are deftly painted in the mind of a prospective buyer through one or more of the five senses.

If these word pictures are not clear and distinct, beautifully harmonized and properly fertilized with motive, they will not move the prospective buyer to action. Professional salespeople paint their pictures in the minds of prospective buyers through as many motives and through as many of the senses as possible. They often supplement mere word pictures with samples or actual pictures of their products, knowing that sales are more easily made when the presentation reaches the mind of the prospective buyer through more than one of the five senses, and also when more than one motive for buying has been planted in the buyer's mind.

Professional salesmanship begins and ends with proper motive. As long as the right motive has been injected into the selling argument, it makes very little difference what happens between the opening and closing of the sale. In a way, all selling is like that. Individuals are moved to buy or not to buy because of motive. Base your sales presentation upon the right motive, and your sale is made before you start. Remember, however, that motive usually must be established in the mind of the prospective buyer; most people have neither the imagination nor the inclination to build their own motives for your product. Only weak-willed people will permit themselves to be sold unless a sufficiently impelling motive has been tactfully but forcefully planted in their minds by the salesperson.

Showmanship is an important factor not only in professional salesmanship but in practically every calling. An efficient showman is one who can dramatize the commonplace events of life and give them the interesting appearance of uniqueness. Efficient showmanship calls for sufficient imagination to be able to recognize things, people, and circumstances that are capable of being dramatized. Through efficient showmanship, economist Roger Babson, founder of Babson College, made a fortune out of dry statistics and monotonous columns of figures. Through the use of graphic charts and appropriate illustrations, he made figures talk. His success was due almost if not entirely to his showmanship ability.

Theodore Roosevelt was one of the most colorful presidents who ever occupied the White House. Although many doubt that he was one of the most brilliant or capable executives, he was popular because he was a master showman; he understood publicity and dramatic values and made use of both effectively. Perhaps Calvin Coolidge had the least colorful personality of any man who ever occupied the White House. He appeared frigid and reserved. John F. Kennedy was vital and enthusiastic; moreover, he understood how to display his magnetism. Kennedy will be remembered and talked about long after Coolidge has been forgotten, because he knew how to dramatize the commonplace and prosaic events of life so they would stand out and attract attention.

Great personalities are remembered. People buy personalities and ideas much more quickly than they buy merchandise. For this very reason, the salesperson who is an efficient showman makes sales where others cannot. The life insurance salesperson who knows nothing about showmanship and does not possess a magnetic personality usually tail-ends the list of producers. Life insurance salespeople who are efficient showmen and possess magnetic personalities seldom mention the word *policy*. They do not have to. They deal in ideas and use them to paint alluring pictures that interest and please prospective buyers. An efficient showman makes effective use of enthusiasm. Poor showmen know nothing of enthusiasm. They trust their case to colorless statements of fact to appeal to the prospective buyer's reason.

Most people are not influenced largely by reason; they are swayed by emotion or feeling. Those who are not capable of deeply arousing their own emotions are not apt to be able to appeal to others through their emotional natures. During the heyday of his career, evangelist Billy Sunday was the greatest showman who ever went gunning for the devil. He could sell tickets into heaven and make the crowd stand in line and like it. The public contributed millions of dollars, while other preachers who lacked a sense of the dramatic starved to death.

Be an able salesperson and you can be almost anything else you wish to be. New York mayor John V.

Lindsay was an efficient showman, which stood above all his other assets. Ex-mayor John F. Hylan was perhaps one of the best mayors New York City ever had, but the least capable in showmanship. The difference in their popularity was the difference between showmanship and the lack of it.

Will Rogers made himself popular through his comments on world news because he had a sufficient sense of the dramatic to make his remarks fit people's moods. That is not merely showmanship; it is salesmanship of the highest order.

Paul Harvey was one of the highest-paid radio commentators in America. He made a fortune through his broadcasts because of his ability to dramatize what people think about or what they wanted to think about and to color the news of the day.

Sales managers who are not efficient showmen are defeated before they begin. They must bring out showmanship qualities in salespeople.

A sales presentation delivered by an able showman is a show all by itself and is as interesting as a play. Moreover, it carries the prospective buyer through exactly the same mental processes as a good play does. Salespeople who are able showmen can change the prospective buyer's mind from negative to positive at will. They accomplish this change not by accident or luck, but by a carefully prearranged plan. An able showman can neutralize the mind of the prospective buyer, regardless of the state of mind the buyer may be in when approached. What is more important, the able showman knows enough not to try to reach a climax or close the sale until this change has been brought about.

The farmer cannot raise wheat without preparing the soil before the seed is sown. A salesperson cannot plant the seed of desire in the prospective buyer's mind while that mind is negative. Salespeople who understand showmanship prepare the mind of the prospective buyer as carefully and scientifically as the farmer prepares the ground. If they do not, they are not salespeople.

A little while ago a salesman walked into a man's office while the man was engaged in a heated argument with his wife over the telephone. When the conversation was finished, the man turned to the salesman and barked, "What the hell do you want?"

Undismayed by the unfortunate moment of his call, the salesman replied with a soft drawl and a kindly grin, "I'm organizing a defense club for husbands," going on to explain that he also had that kind of wife.

The two men talked about women for ten minutes, after which the salesman tactfully switched the talk to his product and went away with a $10,000 sale.

That was showmanship plus salesmanship. The salesman who knew nothing about showmanship would have failed in this case. This salesman, knowing the value of the dramatic, turned an unfortunate situation into an advantage for himself. As Napoleon Hill has said, "With every adversity lies an equal seed of benefit."

Sometimes you must diligently hunt for this benefit. Cookware executive William Burnette converted a sales strategy into $5 million in five years by teaching salespeople how to sell aluminum kitchen utensils. His entire plan can be described in one sentence: he taught his salesmen how to organize clubs of housewives for the purpose of selling them aluminum ware. More specifically, Burnette's plan was to invite the housewives of a community to a luncheon at one of their homes, all expenses paid. The meal was to be cooked by one of his salesmen with the aluminum ware he was selling. After luncheon, the salesman would take orders for the ware, running all the way from $25 to three times that amount.

The sales strategy of the plan turned the trick for Burnette. Because he was a professional salesman, William Burnette lifted himself from the lowly work of house-to-house canvassing, in which he had previously been engaged, to making himself a multimillionaire in five years.

Bear in mind that Burnette's salesmen were selling a complete kitchen set of aluminum ware, not merely a few pots and pans. Also, no individual selling was done. The work consisted of group sales, which took place after the luncheon had been served. The woman at whose home the luncheon was given usually signed the first order, the others quickly falling into line.

As the reader may observe, page after page of this book is devoted to emphasizing the importance of sales strategy or a plan that has been carefully built around the proper motive. One of the major differences between a professional salesperson and the mere sales agent is the fact that the professional is familiar with the nine basic motives and uses at least one of them as a foundation for a selling plan. By contrast, sales agents use neither motive nor plan. They try to sell by main strength and awkwardness through a hit-or-miss method, which sometimes works but usually misses.

We shall soon describe the attributes of a professional salesperson as well as the fundamental rules and principles of salesmanship. The preceding portion of this book has been intended to prepare the reader's mind to assimilate these rules and principles more quickly and to illustrate how they have been applied by those who have attained mastery in selling.

Now we will go on to describe the principles which a successful professional salesperson must know as well as how these principles may be developed and applied most effectively.

Chapter Four

QUALITIES THE PROFESSIONAL
SALESPERSON MUST DEVELOP

Many factors enter into the makeup of the successful salesperson. Most of these are personal in nature and have more to do with the individual than with the products or services he or she sells. We will investigate these factors in detail.

In cultivating the principles here discussed, there are two elements involved. First, a self-searching analysis to determine the presence or absence of these desirable qualities, and second, deliberate effort in cultivating them.

As most so-called mental traits have a physical basis, many of these desired qualities can be attained by doing or attempting to do those things which lead to the desired end. Science has abundantly proved that a state of mind reflects a physical condition and that chemical and physical factors within the body bring about the moods, feelings, and thoughts that academic psychology used to classify as purely mental. Even thought has been proved by scientists, including the great John B. Watson, to be intimately bound up with speech. Therefore talk to yourself about the things you want to take root and grow in your mind and character. This is the very first step, and it is a very profitable step too.

The second principle is like the first in that it is also a physical activity: doing the things that you would like to do. We learn by experience; after all, it is the greatest of all teachers. Habits can be cultivated as well in the mind as in the body, because both mind and body function on a physical plane.

Now, then, what are some of the absolutely necessary things for professional salespeople to have in their mental equipment? There is a list of very desirable qualities which almost any normal and reasonable person can come to possess and exercise. The list is long, and perfection may be only slowly attained. Therefore, before entering into a detailed consideration of the things you would like to have your mind and body capable of doing, let us enumerate those that are absolutely necessary.

1. *Physical fitness* is of tremendous importance, for the simple reason that neither mind nor body can function well without it. Therefore give attention to your

habits of life, proper diet, healthful exercise, and fresh air.

2. *Courage* must be a part of every man or woman who succeeds in any undertaking, especially that of selling in these trying times of intense competition.

3. *Imagination* is an absolute requisite in successful salespeople. They must anticipate situations and even objections on the part of their prospective customers. They must have such a lively imagination as to place themselves in sympathetic understanding with the position, needs, and objectives of the customer. They must almost literally stand in the other's shoes. This takes real imagination.

4. *Speech.* The tone of voice must be pleasing. A highly pitched, squeaky voice is irritating; words half swallowed are hard to understand. Speak distinctly and enunciate clearly. A meek voice indicates a weak person. A firm, clear, clean-cut voice, which moves with assurance and color, indicates a person with enthusiasm and aggressiveness.

5. *Hard work* is the only thing that will turn sales training and ability into money. No amount of good health, courage, or imagination is worth a dime unless it is put to work. The amount of pay salespeople get is usually fixed by the amount of hard and intelligent work that they actually put out. Many people side-step this factor of success.

The above principles are simple; there is nothing unusual or impossible or even striking in them, separately or collectively, unless perhaps it be the fact that most salespeople fail to possess one or more of them. Some salespeople may work hard and even use their imaginations well until they meet a succession of rebuffs and turndowns. It is here that salespeople with soundness in their souls, stamina in their backbones, and courage in their hearts come right back and whip their counterparts who do not have these qualities.

Courage is essential. Then again, many salespeople have been known to possess courage, imagination, and hard work, yet by dissipation and bodily excesses handicap themselves so as to be physically unfit half the time to carry on their work.

Other qualifications considered by experienced sales managers as necessary in the equipment of successful salespeople may be listed as follows:

6. *Knowledge of the merchandise they sell.* Supersalespeople carefully analyze the merchandise or service they sell. They thoroughly understand its every advantage, because they know they cannot successfully sell anything that they themselves do not understand or believe in.

7. *Belief in the merchandise or service.* Supersalespeople never try to sell anything in which they do not have implicit confidence, because they know that their

own minds will broadcast that lack of confidence to the mind of the prospective buyer, regardless of what they may say about their products.

8. *Appropriateness of merchandise.* Supersalespeople analyzes prospective buyers and their needs and offer only what is appropriate to both. They will never try to sell a Rolls-Royce to someone who ought to purchase a Ford, even if the prospective buyer is financially able to buy the more expensive car. They know that a bad bargain for the buyer is a worse bargain for the seller.

9. *Value given.* Supersalespeople never try to get more for their products than they are actually worth, realizing that the sustained confidence and goodwill of the prospective buyer is worth more than a long profit on a single sale.

10. *Knowledge of the prospective buyer.* Supersalespeople are character analysts. They have the ability to ascertain from prospective buyers which of the nine basic motives they will respond to most freely, and they build their sales presentation around those motives. Moreover, if the prospective buyer has no outstanding motive for buying, the supersalesperson creates one, knowing that a motive is essential in closing a sale.

11. *Qualifying the prospective buyer.* Supersalespeople never try to make a sale without properly qualifying

the prospective buyer. In advance of their efforts to close a sale, they inform themselves about the following points: (a) the prospect's financial capacity to purchase; (b) the prospect's need for what is being offered; and (c) the prospect's motive for making the purchase. Endeavoring to make sales without first qualifying the prospective buyer is a mistake that stands at the head of the list of causes for no sale.

12. *Ability to neutralize the mind of the buyer.* Supersalespeople know that no sale can be made until the mind of the prospective buyer has been neutralized or made receptive. Because they know this, they will not endeavor to close a sale until they have opened the mind of the buyer and prepared it as a background upon which they may put together the word mosaic of their story. This is the point where many salespeople fail.

13. *Ability to close a sale.* Supersalespeople are artists at reaching and successfully passing the closing point in selling. They train themselves to sense the psychological moment when a favorable conclusion may be reached successfully. They rarely, if ever, ask prospective buyers if they are ready to purchase. Instead they go on the assumption that the buyer is ready and conduct themselves accordingly in conversation and general demeanor. They use the power of suggestion most effectively.

Supersalespeople avoid trying to close a sale until they know in their own minds that they can close successfully. They so conduct their sales presentations that prospective buyers believe themselves to be the active parties.

Other principles to be acquired have more to do with the personal makeup and self-organization of the salesperson than with his goods. Some of them are:

14. *A pleasing personality*. Supersalespeople have acquired the art of making themselves agreeable to other people, because they know that the prospective buyer must buy the salesperson as well as the merchandise he or she sells, or no sale can be made.

15. *Showmanship*. Supersalespeople are also supershowmen. They have the ability to reach the mind of the prospective buyer by dramatizing the presentation and giving it colors sufficient to arouse intense interest through an appeal to the buyer's imagination.

16. *Self-control*. Supersalespeople exercise complete control over their heads and hearts at all times, knowing that if they do not control themselves, they cannot control the prospective buyer.

17. *Initiative*. Supersalespeople understand the value of initiative. They never have to be told what to do or how to do it. Having a keen imagination, they use it and create plans which they translate into action

through their own initiative. They need but little supervision and, generally speaking, are given none.

18. *Tolerance*. Supersalespeople are open-minded and tolerant on all subjects, knowing that open-mindedness is essential for growth.

19. *Accurate thinking*. Supersalespeople think. Moreover, they take the time and go to the trouble to gather facts as the basis for thinking. They do no guessing when facts are available. They have no set or immovable opinions that are not based upon what they know to be facts.

20. *Persistence*. Supersalespeople are never influenced by the word *no*, and they do not recognize the word *impossible*. To them, all things are possible of achievement. To them, the word *no* is nothing more than a signal to begin the sales presentation in earnest. They know that all buyers take the line of least resistance by resorting to the *no* alibi. Because they have this knowledge, they are not susceptible to negative influence by sales resistance.

21. *Faith*. Supersalespeople have superfaith in: (a) the products they are selling; (b) themselves; (c) the prospective buyer; and (d) closing the sale. They never try to make a sale without the aid of faith, because they know that faith is contagious: it is picked up through the receiving station of the prospective buyer's mind. Without the quality of faith, there can be no super-

salesmanship. Faith is a state of mind which may be described as an intensified form of self-reliance. It has been said that faith moves mountains, but it also makes sales.

22. *The habit of observation.* Supersalespeople are close observers of small details. Every word uttered by the prospective buyer, every change of facial expression, every movement is observed and its significance weighed accurately. Supersalespeople not only observe and analyze accurately all that the prospective buyer does and says but also make deductions from what the prospect does *not* do or say. Nothing escapes the supersaleperson's attention.

23. *The habit of rendering more service than is expected.* Supersalespeople follow the habit of rendering service that is greater in quantity and finer in quality than they are expected to render, thereby profiting from the law of increasing returns as well as the law of compensation.

24. *Profiting by failures and mistakes.* Supersalespeople regard nothing as lost effort. They profit by all of their mistakes and by observing the mistakes of others. They know that in every failure and mistake may be found, if analyzed, the seed of an equivalent success.

25. *The Master Mind.* Supersalespeople understand and apply the Master Mind principle, through which they greatly multiply their power to achieve. The

Master Mind principle means the coordination of two or more individual minds working in perfect harmony for a definite purpose. The Master Mind will be discussed in more detail in chapter 6.

26. *A definite major aim.* Supersalespeople always work with a definite sales quota or goal in mind. They never go at their work merely with the aim of selling all they can. They not only work with a definite goal in mind, but set a definite time in which to attain that goal. The psychological effect of a definite chief aim will be described in chapter 5, on autosuggestion.

27. *The Golden Rule applied.* Supersalespeople use the Golden Rule as the foundation for all of business transactions, putting themselves in the other person's shoes and seeing the situation from the other's viewpoint.

Of all the qualities that a salesperson must possess, none is more necessary, none more valuable than this next one:

28. *Enthusiasm.* Supersalespeople have an abundance of enthusiasm, which they can use at will. They know the vibrations of thought that they release through their enthusiasm will be picked up by the prospective buyer and acted upon as if it were the prospect's own creation. Enthusiasm is a difficult thing to explain,

but its presence is always easily recognized. Everybody likes enthusiastic people. They are high of spirit and radiate an atmosphere of good fellowship, high faith, and lofty purpose. Perhaps their enthusiasm is born of their own deep faith in themselves, the mission of their work, and the good they do.

Enthusiasm in people, and the lack of it, may be compared to the light that surrounds a flashing diamond on a jeweler's tray. Its spontaneity and iridescence compel admiration and give value to it in contrast to the dull, leaden atmosphere surrounding a piece of glass the same size. The glass can be bought for a song (with none willing to sing it), while the diamond is eagerly sought by all, great and small, rich and poor. Therefore to every salesperson, this advice is given, as though from Sinai: "With all thy getting, get enthusiasm."

Mastery and connection with these major factors entitle sellers to rate as supersalespeople. If you aspire to mastery in selling, study this list carefully and make sure you are not weak in any of these qualities.

You will observe that every quality may be acquired. This does not harmonize with a false notion, held by some people, that salespeople are born and not made. Salesmanship is an art and a science and may be acquired by those with the will to acquire it. Some people are blessed with personalities which are favorable to quick mastery of the factors of supersalesmanship, while others must develop such a personality, but it can be developed.

There are nine basic motives to which people respond most freely. Science is cataloguing the responses of which normal people are capable and has set forth for us the types of appeal that will induce desired responses. Responses may be of a low grade, such as scientists would call purely the results of physics, or which are prompted by physiochemical stimuli. You may cause someone to get out of the office by kicking him out: that's purely physical. Or he may be induced to act by reason of those chemical reactions incident to a peculiar condition of the physical body, temperature, atmosphere, and physical comfort or discomforts, as well as food and drink. These bring about chemical conditions that prompt certain reactions.

But forgetting these more elementary and purely physical responses, we may classify the appeals that induce appropriate responses under three heads. These are the only ones we need address here. They are: (1) appeals to instinct; (2) appeals to emotion; and (3) appeals to reason. The appeals that cause most people to buy food, clothing, and shelter fall primarily into the first group, though in a lesser degree they may find a field of expression in the other two.

All things in the world that are desirable because of their beauty may be sold because of suitable appeals made under the second heading: emotion. Love, marriage, and religion, for instance, deal largely in emotional appeals. Many goods and services are also sold on emotional appeal, including education, books, the theater, music, art, life insurance, advertising, cosmetics, toys, and luxuries.

Investments, savings, mechanical appliances, business machines, and scientific works often change hands on appeals to reason.

There are nine basic motives to which people respond and by one or more of which they are influenced in practically every thought and deed. When supersalespeople qualify prospective buyers, they look first for the most logical motive that will influence their minds.

The nine basic motives, listed in the approximate order of their importance and usefulness, are:

1. Self-preservation
2. Financial gain
3. Love
4. The sex urge
5. Desire for power and fame
6. Fear
7. Revenge
8. Freedom of body and mind
9. Desire to build and to create, both in thought and in the material realm

Supersalespeople check their presentations against these nine basic motives to make sure that they embrace and appeal through as many of them as possible. They know that a sales presentation is more effective when based upon more than one motive. No salesperson has any right to try to sell anything to anyone without presenting through their sales argument a logical motive for the purchaser to buy, and no supersalesperson will try to do so.

Supersalesmanship contemplates the rendering of useful service to the buyer. High-pressure methods do not come within the category of supersalesmanship, mainly because such methods presuppose the lack of a logical motive for buying. The very fact that high-pressure methods are employed is evidence that the person doing the selling has no logical motive to offer the prospective purchaser as to why he or she should buy. High-pressure salespeople usually depend upon superlatives to take the place of motives for buying. This is a form of hijacking to which professional salespeople never resort. If your sales presentation plan does not emphasize one or more of the nine basic motives, it is weak and should be revised.

Careful analysis of over thirty thousand salespeople revealed that the outstanding weaknesses of approximately 98 percent of them were to be found among the following weaknesses in technique:

1. Failure to present a motive for buying
2. Lack of persistence in sales presentation and closing
3. Failure to quantify prospective buyers
4. Failure to neutralize the minds of prospective buyers
5. Lack of imagination
6. Absence of enthusiasm

These deficiencies are common among the majority of salespeople in all fields. Any one of these weaknesses is sufficient to destroy the chances of a sale. You will observe that failure to present a motive for buying heads this list. Nothing but indifference or lack of knowledge of scientific selling could explain this, the major weakness in the personality and habits of salespeople.

Success in selling is the result of positive qualities which one must possess and use. Failure in selling is the result of negative qualities, which should be eliminated. Among the more outstanding negative qualities are the following:

1. *The habit of procrastination.* There is no substitute for prompt and persistent action.

2. *One or more of the six basic fears.* Those whose minds are filled with any form of fear cannot sell success-fully. The six basic fears are: (a) the fear of poverty; (b) the fear of criticism; (c) the fear of ill-health; (d) the fear of loss of someone's love; (e) the fear of

old age; (f) the fear of death. To this list should perhaps be added fear of the prospective buyer.

3. *Spending too much time making calls instead of sales.* A
call is not an interview. An interview is not a sale.
Some who call themselves salespeople have not
learned this truth.

4. *Shifting responsibility to the sales manager.* Sales managers are not supposed to go with a salesperson to
make calls. They do not have enough hours or legs to
do this. Their business is to tell the salesperson what
to do, not to do it for him or her.

5. *Perfection and creating alibis.* Explanations do not
explain; orders do. Nothing else does. Don't forget
that.

6. *Spending too much time in coffee shops.* A coffee shop
is a fine place to park, but the salesperson who parks
there too long is bound to get walking papers sooner
or later.

7. *Buying hard-luck stories instead of selling merchandise.*
Economic conditions are a common topic of discus-
sion, but don't let the purchasing agent use them to
switch your mind from your own story.

8. *Drinking too freely the night before.* Parties are exciting,
but they do not add to the following day's business.

9. *Depending on the sales manager for prospects.* Order takers expect prospective buyers to be hog-tied and held
down until they arrive. Professional salespeople catch

their own prospects on the wing. This is one of the chief reasons why they are professional salespeople.

10. *Waiting for business conditions to pick up.* Business is always good with the robins, but they do not wait for someone to dig the worms out of the ground. Be at least as clever as a robin. Orders are not being slipped under salespeople's doors this year or any other year.

11. *Hearing the word* no. To a real salesperson, this word is only a signal to begin fighting. If every buyer said yes, salespeople would have no jobs: they would not be needed.

12. *Fearing competition.* Ford has plenty of competition, but they apparently do not fear it, because they have had the courage and the ability to turn out a compact car at an amazingly low price during a period in which many motor manufacturers were not eager to compete against foreign compacts.

13. *Devoting too much time to the poultry business.* The only sort of chickens which lay eggs are the feathered variety, and they roost on farms, not on Broadway or Main Street.

14. *Reading the stock market reports.* Let the suckers bite at this bait. You may be smart enough to dodge the hook, but think how the sales manager would feel if you won a fortune on the stock market and quit the house, as one out of every ten thousand who played the market do sometimes.

15. *Plain pessimism.* That habit of expecting that the prospective buyer will give you the gate is likely to result in your getting it. Life has a clear way of trying to please. It usually gives that which is expected.

This is not a complete list of don'ts, but it is a fair sample. Perhaps some may regard the list as a little too personal and flippant. Others may see in it a touch of sarcasm. It was intended only for those who have corns on their toes; others will not be offended.

If you have any doubt about whether or not you're suffering from any of these don'ts, pick up courage and check the list over with your sales manager. Emphasize that you want him or her to be perfectly frank with you.

This list of don'ts is not original with us. It was compiled from observation of more than three hundred thousand salespeople whom we have had the privilege of training, and some of whom we have directed. Notice that that not one of these don'ts is an attribute of a pleasing personality.

Chapter Five

AUTOSUGGESTION:
THE FIRST STEP IN SALESMANSHIP

Every supersalesperson knows that every sale is made to the salesperson first, and that the extent to which the salesperson makes this sale perfectly measures the degree of conviction that can be induced in the buyer's mind.

Because of the importance of self-selling, autosuggestion assumes an important role in teaching salesmanship. This is the principle through which the salesperson saturates their own mind with belief in the commodity or service offered for sale, as well as in their own ability to sell.

Autosuggestion is self-suggestion. It is the principle by which one imparts to one's subconscious mind any idea, plan, concept, or belief. The subconscious mind is the broadcasting station that voluntarily telegraphs one's thoughts and beliefs, or disbeliefs, to others. Supersalespeople know that they must educate their subconscious minds to broadcast belief in what they are offering for sale. Repetition of a suggestion to one's subconscious mind is the most effective way of educating it to broadcast only such thoughts as will be beneficial.

The subconscious mind will not be influenced by any suggestions made to it, except those which are mixed with feeling or emotion. The head, or the cold reasoning faculty, has no influence whatsoever on the subconscious mind. It responds only to the impulses of thought that have been well mixed with feeling.

The subconscious mind is influenced by the negatives as readily as by the positives. Supersalespeople never overlook this fact. This is one reason they are supersalespeople.

The seven major positive emotions:

1. Sex is placed at the head of a list because it is the most powerful emotion.
2. Love.
3. Hope.
4. Faith.
5. Enthusiasm.
6. Optimism.
7. Loyalty.

The world is controlled by the emotional faculty. Most of our activities from birth until death are induced by our feelings. Salespeople who appeal to buyers through their emotions or feelings will make ten sales to one made by those who appeal through reason alone. Buyers generally make purchases because of some motive that is closely associated with the emotions, as one may readily discern by studying the table of motives that prompt people to buy.

In the foregoing list of seven major positive emotions, supersalespeople will find nature's elixir, which they must mix with the suggestions they plant in their subconscious minds if they expect to broadcast to prospective customers thought impulses that will influence them in favor of the sale.

The seven major negative emotions:

1. Anger, quick and transitory.
2. Fear, prominent and easily discernible.
3. Greed, subtle and persistent.
4. Jealousy, impulsive and spasmodic.
5. Revenge, subtle and quiet.
6. Hatred, subtle and persistent.
7. Superstition, subtle and slow.

The presence of any one of these emotional impulses in the conscious mind is sufficient to discourage the presence of all of the positive emotions. In extreme cases, the presence of a combination of these emotions in the conscious mind may lead to insanity.

Obviously any suggestion planted in the subconscious mind while any one or more of these negative emotions is present will carry with it a coloring of a negative nature. When the subconscious mind broadcasts any such suggestion, it will register a negative result in the minds of those who pick up the vibration. Understand this principle, and you will know why supersalespeople must first sell themselves before trying to sell others.

You will also know why negative-minded salespeople hear *no* so often. Feelings, beliefs, and thoughts released by their subconscious minds speak more loudly than words. Remember that people are motivated either to buy or not to buy through their feelings. Remember also that much of what they believe to be their own feelings actually consists of thought impulses that they have unconsciously picked up from thought vibrations released by the salesperson.

Supersalespeople neither permit their subconscious minds to broadcast negative thoughts nor give expression to them through words, because they understand that like attracts like and negative suggestions attract negative actions and negative decisions from prospective purchasers. The salesperson who knocks anything or anyone thereby destroys the advantage they might obtain through positive suggestion.

The presence in the mind of even one of the negative emotions tends to attract to it a flock of its relatives. Knowing this, the supersalesperson takes care not to plant negative thoughts in the minds of prospective purchasers.

Politics and most politicians are in ill repute all over the country today. Analyze the brand of salesmanship they use and you may readily understand why they have lost the confidence of their buyers. It is customary for those who seek office to do so by attacking their competitors for office instead of selling themselves to the voters on their own merits.

No well-managed business will permit salespeople to seek patronage by knocking competitors. Sales managers have enough common sense to know that sales made by belittling competitors or competitive merchandise are not really sales and that business obtained in this way is a liability in the long run. Political speeches are, as a rule, fine examples of this sort of salesmanship.

A wise philosopher once said that whom the gods would destroy, they first make mad. Anger is a negative emotion; it makes a very poor sale when mixed with salesmanship, whether or not there be just cause for anger. Silence is far more effective than words inspired by and mixed with the emotion of anger. Satire, sarcasm, and negative thoughts expressed by innuendo may give a salesperson a reputation as a wisecracker, but they will not aid him or her in selling products. Out-and-out statements of a negative nature are the equivalent of suicide in selling.

The taxicab companies in New York City engaged in a price war some time ago. The public resented their tactics and registered its resentment through a loss to the business of over $2 million in one year. It used to be a popular pastime for automobile salespeople to endeavor to make sales by knocking competitive cars. More than a hundred automobile manufacturers were forced to the wall before they woke up to the fact that anything which hurts one individual's business hurts all business in that line.

Life insurance men used to follow the practice of twisting—inducing the owner of a policy of a competitive company to give up that policy and purchase one from their company. Intelligent life insurance officials stopped the practice, except in isolated cases. With most life insurance companies, twisting is considered the equivalent of a discharge: agents who do it will not be tolerated any longer than is required to find them out. In fact, there are laws that have been passed to prevent this.

Negative statements in selling not only set up resentment in the minds of the prospective buyer but magnetize the salesperson's own subconscious mind so that it throws off negative vibrations. Other people pick up on these and act upon them to the salesperson's detriment.

Never in the history of the world has there been such abundant opportunity as there is now for the person who is willing to serve before trying to collect.

Chapter Six

THE MASTER MIND

In selling, as in every walk of life, noteworthy achievement is predicated upon power. Power is acquired through organized and intelligently directed knowledge. The Master Mind principle makes available unlimited sources of knowledge, because one may, through its application, avail oneself of the knowledge possessed by others, as well as all knowledge which has been accumulated and recorded in books.

The term *Master Mind* means the coordination of two or more minds working in perfect harmony for a definite purpose. There are two separate and distinct phases of this principle. One is economic in nature, the other psychic. Through the aid of the economic phase, it is obvious that one may through friendly alliance with others avail oneself of their knowledge, experience, and cooperation.

The psychic, spiritual phase leads in an entirely different direction. This portion of the Master Mind principle may be used to connect one's conscious thinking mind with the higher forces of infinite intelligence. Unfortunately, limited space here makes it impractical to describe in detail the psychic phase of the Master Mind. This principle has been fully covered in the Philosophy of Success.

Let us keep in mind the fact that power is essential for successful achievement in every walk of life. Also let us remember that power is organized and intelligently directed knowledge. These facts clearly indicate that power in great quantities can be accumulated only through the coordinated efforts of a plurality of minds. No one individual, functioning independently, no matter how intelligent or well-informed, can ever possess great power. Because power must be transmitted before it is effective, any one individual is limited in the amount of power he or she can transmit or apply.

The student should gain a clear understanding of the two phases of the Master Mind principle given at the outset of this chapter, even if they seem more abstract than concrete. The Master Mind principle is the basis of all great, enduring power. It must therefore be understood and applied by all who attain to mastery in any calling, in selling as well as in other vocations.

Henry Ford began one of the most efficient Master Mind groups known in the entire field of distribution. This group consists of the thousands of trained dealers who operate in practically every part of the world. Through the cooperative efforts of this dealer alliance, the company can estimate, well in advance of the actual building of its cars, how many can be distributed. It knows where the market exists and the extent of that market even before the raw materials for the cars have been assembled. Ford's greatest asset was his Master Mind sales alliance. This is an indisputable fact. Mr. Ford owed his stupendous success to his understanding and application of the Master Mind principle.

Andrew Carnegie first brought the Master Mind principle to Napoleon Hill's attention. Carnegie attributed his huge fortune to his use of it. His Master Mind group consisted of about twenty men, his executive staff, whose combined technical knowledge and experience enabled him to make and market steel successfully. Mr. Carnegie informed Hill that he could have made his fortune in groceries, banking, or railroads or in any business which rendered useful service to a large number of people just as easily as he made it in steel merely by surrounding himself with men whose knowledge and temperament were suited to the pursuit of the business.

The Master Mind principle is the basis of every great fortune: even inherited fortunes were originally accumulated through the Master Mind principle. Successful achievement is the result of power. Power in great quantities can be accumulated only through application of the Master Mind principle. This point must be emphasized, because it contains the very warp and woof of mastery and achievement.

Chapter Seven

CONCENTRATION

Only through the principle of concentration can the psychic phase of the Master Mind principle be reached and used. Concentration is the focusing of the attention, interest, and desire upon the attainment of a definite end. Concentration is essential for the effective use of the Master Mind principle. The two are inseparable when practical results are to be obtained through their use by two or more people.

Autosuggestion or self-suggestion is the principle through which the subconscious mind may be reached and influenced. Concentration is the principle through which autosuggestion must be applied—a fact that has been clearly illustrated in the chapter on that subject. We have termed it the first step in salesmanship.

Let us state these important facts in another way: the Master Mind principle, the principle of concentration, and the principle of autosuggestion constitute a triumvirate that must be used in reaching and influencing the subconscious mind. The subconscious mind will not recognize or be influenced by any suggestion unless that suggestion is mixed with one or more of the emotions mentioned in the previous chapter.

Thus these three principles—the Master Mind, autosuggestion, and concentration—constitute the very heart of professional salesmanship. If you fail to understand and assimilate these three principles, this book will have lost much of its value.

This chapter describes the method for effectively applying the principle of concentration. Don't fail to make the most of it: it is of supreme importance to you.

Concentration is defined as the habit of planting in the mind a definite aim, object, or purpose and visualizing the same until ways and means for its realization have been created. The principle of concentration embraces planting in one's conscious mind a definite chief aim, idea, plan, or purpose and continuously focusing on it with the conscious mind.

The principle of concentration is the medium by which procrastination is overcome. The same principle is the foundation upon which both self-confidence and self-control are predicated. Habit and concentration go hand in glove. Habit may grow out of concentration, and concentration may grow out of habit. The object of concentrating upon a definite aim is to train the mind until it forms the habit of focusing upon the object of that aim. By focusing upon one's definite aim through concentrated effort and attention, this habit comes to influence the aim and translates it into its physical counterpart through the most practical and direct methods available.

One thing you must remember when you live this philosophy: your mind is in the future, while your body waits to catch up. Once, when a man started talking about his Rolls-Royce, a few of his friends didn't understand that the Rolls-Royce had been purchased in the man's mind but would not be purchased physically until a few months later.

Every human being makes use of the principle of concentration, whether he realizes it or not. The person who permits the conscious mind to dwell upon the negative thoughts of fear, poverty, ill-health, and intolerance thereby applies the law of concentration. Sooner or later the subconscious mind will pick up the suggestions, act upon them, and translate them into their physical counterparts.

Instructions for applying concentration:

1. Master and apply the principles described in the chapter on autosuggestion by following the habit of giving orders to your subconscious mind, mixing

your thoughts with one or more of the positive emotions, and repeating your orders over and over. Keep
up this procedure until you get satisfactory results,
remembering that eternal vigilance is the price of
mastery.

2. Empty your conscious mind of all other thoughts.
After a little practice, you will be able to focus your
mind entirely upon any subject that you please. The
act of focusing upon one subject and keeping your
mind upon that one subject is concentration.

3. Hold your thoughts to the object of your concentration with a burning desire for the attainment of
whatever object you have in mind. When concentrating upon your definite chief aim, do so in perfect
faith that you will realize the object of that aim.

4. When you find your conscious mind wavering, drive
it back and focus it upon that subject again and again
until you have developed such perfect self-control
that you can keep all other thoughts out of your
mind. Mix emotions or feeling with your thoughts
when concentrating; otherwise they will not be recognized by your subconscious mind.

5. The principle of concentration may be best applied in
an environment of silence, where there are no counter-
attractions or noises of any disturbing nature. The
best time for concentrating is after you have retired at
night, when the number of distractions is minimized.

6. Your subconscious mind can best be reached and influenced when you concentrate your conscious mind upon an idea, plan, or purpose in a spirit of intense enthusiasm, because enthusiasm arouses your faculty of creative imagination and puts it into action.

Any idea, plan, purpose, or definite aim that you persistently submit to your subconscious mind through the medium of concentration brings to your aid the force of infinite intelligence, until eventually practical plans of procedure will flash into your mind during your period of concentration.

When you first start your practice of concentration, you may not experience the feeling that you are in communication with a superior intelligence. But in time, if you develop the habit of regular concentration, you will be thoroughly cognizant of the fact that a superior intelligence is influencing you. It is a well-known fact that the jack-of-all-trades never achieves success. Life is very complicated, and there are so many ways of dissipating energy unprofitably that the habit of concentrated effort must be formed and adhered to by all who succeed.

Power is predicated upon organized energy. Energy can only be organized through concentration. It is a fact worthy of serious consideration that all individuals of outstanding success in all walks of life are those who concentrate the major portion of their thoughts and efforts upon some one definite purpose or chief aim. By analyzing the principle of the Master Mind, you will observe that when two or more people ally themselves in a spirit of harmony for the purpose of achieving some definite object, that alliance functions through the principle of concentrated effort.

From our analysis of more than seventy-five thousand men and women who were rated as failures, we observed that not one of these followed the habit of focusing his or her mind upon a definite chief aim using concentration.

The thirty major causes of failure may be either controlled or eliminated entirely through the principle of concentration, indicating the importance of this principle as a part of the working equipment of the successful salesperson.

Nearly everyone has a definite chief aim at one time or another; 95 percent of the people who have such aims, however, make no attempt to realize them, because they have not learned the art of concentrating on their definite aims for sufficient lengths of time to fix these aims in the subconscious mind. The majority of the people who adopt definite aims do so more in the nature of a wish than in the form of a definite, determined, and well defined intention. Merely permitting a definite aim to come into one's mind is in no way beneficial. To be of permanent value, such an aim must be fixed in the mind through concentration.

Concentration develops the power of persistence and enables one to master all forms of temporary defeat. The majority of people have never learned the real difference between temporary defeat and permanent failure because they lack the persistence necessary to stage a comeback after they have experienced temporary defeat. Persistence is merely concentrated effort well mixed with determination and faith.

From these facts you will readily understand that the principle of a definite chief aim and the principle of concentration are complementary: one can be applied successfully only with the aid of the other. Every human being is ruled by the law of habit. Because this is true, those who learn to build their habits to order control the major cause of successful achievement. Concentration is the principle through which one build one's habits to order. It has been correctly said that we first make our habits, and our habits then make us.

We have habits of mind and habits of body; both are subject to control, and the medium of that control is concentration. The mind is just as susceptible to the influence of habit as is the physical body. Through concentration, we may force the mind to dwell upon any subject we desire until the mind falls into the habit of dwelling on that subject. It then follows the habit automatically.

There is no point of compromise between us and our habits: either we control our habits or they control us.

Successful individuals, understanding this truth, force themselves to build the sort of habits by which they are willing to be controlled. Habits are formed step-by-step through our every thought and deed. Center your thoughts upon a definite aim through concentration, and very soon your subconscious mind will pick up a clear picture of that aim and aid you in translating it into its physical counterpart.

All thought has a tendency to externalize itself. This is a truth well known to every psychologist, as it was known to him who wrote, "Whatsoever a man soweth, that shall he also reap." Your financial condition is not the result of chance or accident. It reflects perfectly the nature of your dominating thoughts, desires, and aims. An analysis of those who have accumulated huge fortunes has revealed in every case that they represented the consummation of the state of mind of those who had accumulated them.

The person who understands the possibilities of concentration need rarely know the word *impossible*. This book has repeatedly made reference to the power of infinite intelligence. If such a power can be influenced to inject itself into our affairs and made to help us achieve the object of our aims and purposes, it is certain that this stupendous result can be attained only through the principle of concentration.

We owe eternal allegiance to infinite intelligence. No church or creed would quarrel with such an attitude. This statement is made for the sole purpose of enabling every reader to become more familiar with a great universal law, which is capable of being harnessed and induced to separate humans from all causes of doubt, worry, and fear.

There is definitely a power in prayer. We can define a prayer as any fixed or definite aim that is founded upon faith in the realization of that aim. Concentration without faith appears to bring no results, but concentration *with* faith appears to achieve results that border on the miraculous. Yet faith without action is of no avail. The process of mixing faith with a definite chief aim is one which is indeed difficult to describe and more difficult still to apply. Faith can only be induced through concentration upon the object of one's hopes, aims, and purposes.

Napoleon Hill visited with department store magnate F. W. Woolworth a little while before Mr. Woolworth's death, and in these words he described the method through which he built what was at that time the tallest building in the world: "I had an architect draw up a set of plans. Every day for more than six months, I went into my private office, shut the door, and looked over these plans for more than half an hour. Each time that I looked at them, the actual physical building seemed nearer a reality. Finally, the day came when the exact method by which I financed the Woolworth Building flashed into my mind, and I knew instantly that the building was a reality. From that point on, I had no difficulty whatsoever."

New York's Woolworth Building became a reality because F. W. Woolworth concentrated upon that building until concentrated thought externalized itself in physical reality.

Writing in *The Christian Science Monitor*, Mr. Willis J. Abbot said:

A while ago, I was in the original Menlo Park laboratory of Edison, which Henry Ford with pious reverence for the great inventor had erected at Dearborn, Michigan. All the earlier tools of Edison's craft are there; the first electric incandescent light (it had a life of eight hours); the first phonograph, on which a needle playing over a tinfoil recorded and emitted a squeaky imitation of the human voice. Thousands of bottles of chemicals lined the walls.

Mr. Edison had to have every known chemical where he could put his hand on it, said the custodian who had worked with him half a century ago. But to me, more interesting than the material relics was a picture the custodian drew for me, little thinking how impressive it was. "Often Mr. Ford comes in here," he said. "He pulls up that chair and just sits and thinks. Sometimes he will sit almost an hour and then go out without a word to anyone."

What are the thoughts of the giant of industrial organization as he sits thus surrounded by the relics of the earlier triumphs of Edison's wizardry? Thinking, he once said, "is the hardest work that any man can do." Perhaps he found it easier to think out his problems in an environment which had witnessed the solution of so many. At any rate, the spectacle of Henry Ford, thus plunged in meditation, amidst the evidences of Edison's struggles and victories, is one to challenge thought.

It is difficult for anyone to say which of the principles described in this course is the most important, but concentration may be the keystone to the arch of the whole subject. Chinn Ho, the wealthiest man in Hawaii, whose father had worked in the fields, was asked for his secret for success. His answer was having a chief goal and concentrating on it.

Your employer does not control the sort of service you render; you control that, and it is the thing that makes or breaks you.

Chapter Eight

INITIATIVE AND LEADERSHIP

Initiative means doing things without being told to do them. It means selecting a definite aim and building plans for its achievement. Its most profitable application is in the selection of a Master Mind group. If you use judgment in the selection of this group, your Master Mind alliance will give you the power of real leadership.

In applying initiative and leadership, certain definite steps are essential. Following are the most important of these steps:

1. Know definitely what you want.
2. Build a practical plan or plans for the achievement of that which you want, making use of the counsel and advice of your Master Mind group.

3. Surround yourself with an organization made up of individuals who have the knowledge and experience essential for carrying out your definite aim.

4. Have sufficient faith in yourself and in your plans to see your aim a finished reality even before you begin to carry out your plans.

5. Don't become discouraged, no matter what obstacles you may encounter. If one plan fails to work, substitute other plans until you have found the one that will work.

6. Don't guess, but get facts as the basis for all of your plans.

7. Don't be influenced by others to abandon your plans or your aim.

8. Have no set hours for work. Leaders must devote to their tasks whatever hours are necessary for success.

9. Concentrate upon one thing at a time so you won't dissipate thought and energy.

10. Whenever possible, relegate to others the responsibility for details, but have a system for checking your subordinates to see that these details are accurately attended to. Hold yourself accountable at all times for carrying out all of your plans, bearing in mind that if subordinates fail, it is you yourself who have failed.

Persistence is the keynote to success for all great leaders. If you're going to become discouraged at the first signs of opposition or adversity, you will never become a great leader. Leadership means the capacity to assume great responsibility. If you lack the quality of persistence, be sure your Master Mind group has at least one person who has this quality.

Efficient leaders never permit themselves to be loaded down with small details. They have the ability to so organize their plans that they are free at all times to place the weight of their personal effort wherever it is most needed. Of the most able industrial leaders of America, not one of these ever seemed rushed with work, for the simple reason that in every case the responsibility of details had been relegated to others.

Those who boast of the habit of inspecting personally all the details of their business either are not able leaders or are at the head of a very small business.

"I haven't had time," is said to be the most dangerous sentence in the English language. Anyone who makes such an admission confesses his or her lack of ability as a leader. The real leader has time for everything necessary for successful leadership.

The stock alibi of more than 90 percent of the world's failures, who have not selected a definite chief aim in life, is, "I just haven't had time to get around to it."

An efficient leader is not necessarily the person who appears to be the busiest, but the person who can so organize plans that he or she can efficiently direct and keep large numbers of subordinates busy. The individual who can get things done is much more profitable to a business than the individual who actually does the work.

Efficient leaders are also efficient salespeople. They get other to do things because they wish to. Efficient leaders have pleasing personalities. They are optimistic and enthusiastic, and they know how to transmit this enthusiasm and optimism to their followers. An efficient leader is courageous. No one wishes to follow a leader who is lacking in courage, and in fact will not do so.

The efficient leader has a keen sense of justice and deals with followers fairly and justly. An efficient leader assumes full responsibility for the acts of subordinates. If they make mistakes, he assumes that it is he that has really made the mistake, because it was he who chose the subordinates. The efficient leader understands the rules of pedagogy and is an able teacher. An efficient leader reaches decisions quickly and changes them slowly.

There are circumstances, of course, which call for slow deliberation and the examination of facts before an intelligent decision can be reached. However, after all the available facts have been gathered and organized, there is no excuse for delaying decision, and the person who practices the habit of delay cannot become an effective leader without mastering this shortcoming.

For more than a hundred years, there had been talk about the building of the Panama Canal, but the actual work of building the canal never got much beyond the talk stage until Theodore Roosevelt became president of the United States. With the firmness of decision that was the very warp and woof of his achievements and the real basis of his reputation as a leader, Roosevelt took the initiative, had a bill framed for Congress to pass, provided for the appropriation, organized his Master Mind group of engineers, and went to work with a spirit of self-confidence. The much talked of Panama Canal became a splendid reality. We have had more learned men than Theodore Roosevelt in the White House, but we have had few who were greater leaders.

Leaders are men of action. General Grant said, "We will fight it out on this line if it takes all summer," and despite his many other deficiencies, he stood by that decision and won. On the other side, the Civil War would have lasted weeks instead of years without the capable leaders of the Confederacy.

When asked by one of his sailors what he would do if they saw no signs of land by the following day, Columbus replied, "If we see no land tomorrow, we will sail on and on." He too had a definite chief aim and a plan for its attainment. And he too had reached the decision not to quit or to turn back until success had crowned his efforts. Columbus was a man with great ability as a leader.

Napoleon, when surprised by the enemy, having discovered that there was a deep camouflaged ditch just ahead of the line of march, gave orders for his cavalry to charge the ditch. He waited until the dead bodies of men and horses filled the ditch, then marched his troops across and whipped the enemy.

That required instantaneous decision. One minute of faltering or hesitation, and he would have been outflanked by the enemy and captured. He did the unexpected or impossible. His capacity to act quickly without waiting to be told by others what to do was the quality that marked him as a great leader. It was said that to outflank Napoleon would take horses with wings.

President Kennedy, when confronted with the Cuban Missile Crisis, took a firm stand, and will go down in history as the first president since World War II who made the communists back down.

The first essential step to the development of initiative and leadership is forming the habit of prompt and firm decision. That great leader must have a tremendous capacity for quick and prompt decision. Individuals who hesitate between vague notions of what they want to or should do generally end up doing nothing.

This is an age when initiative and leadership are in demand in practically every calling. Never in the history of the world have these qualities meant so much as they do today, because millions of people throughout the world are in an unsettled, undecided state of mind. In America, the doors are wide open to individuals who have the qualities of initiative and leadership in states-manship, religion, industry, finance, transportation, merchandising, education, and a score of other lines of endeavor. At the present time there are few outstanding people in any of these fields.

There is a mistaken notion in the world that people are paid for what they know. This is only partly true and, like other half-truths, it does more damage than an out-and-out falsehood. The truth is, people are paid not merely for what they know, but more particularly for what they do with what they know or what they can get others to do.

In a letter, one man said, "I have a splendid education, and I could be a great success, if someone would only show me what to do and how to do it." Successful people never wait for others to show them what to do or how to do it. They take the initiative themselves, appoint themselves to leadership, enlist the necessary assistance and capital, and forge ahead despite all opposition.

Self-confidence is essential for success in leadership. One natural tendency of human nature is a willingness to follow the individual with great self-confidence. No one wishes to follow leaders who do not seem to be sure of themselves. It was said of Napoleon that his soldiers would willingly follow him to their deaths because of his example of courage and self-confidence.

A real leader is always persistent and never accepts temporary defeat as failure. Leaders who often change their minds lose the confidence of their followers. They let it be known that they are not sure of themselves. If they aren't, how can they expect their followers to be sure of them?

Real leaders show no partiality among followers. If they have friends or relatives in the organization, they treat them exactly like the rest of the staff.

A real leader not only has self-reliance and courage personally but imparts these qualities to subordinates. When Cyrus H. K. Curtis placed a man in charge of one of his publications, he said to him, "I am turning this property over to you to be managed and run just exactly as if you had the legal title to it. Make your own decisions, select your own help, create your own policy, lay out your own plans, and then accept the entire responsibility for its success. All I wish to see is a satisfactory balance sheet at the end of the year."

Mr. Curtis was one of the most successful publishers in the world. He was successful because he himself was a great leader, and his leadership was based primarily upon his understanding of the principle of relegating responsibility to others. He would not permit his subordinates to shift any responsibility back to him. In this way he created efficient leaders.

The president of the United States would get nowhere if he undertook to instruct all of his associates how to plan and conduct their campaigns. He places on their shoulders the responsibility of planning and carrying out their plans. The able business leader must also do this. People always do their best work when they feel they are acting upon their own initiative and know they must assume full responsibility for their actions. There can be no real leadership in any calling without assumption of responsibility. We all want to be leaders in one way or another. Most of us would like to have the authority and the pay that belongs to the individual who tells other people what to do, but few of us wish to accept the responsibility that goes with that authority.

Real leaders have no set hours of labor, for no other reason than that it is their business to carry out their plans no matter how many hours may be required for the task. Real leaders make due allowance for the ordinary weaknesses of their subordinates and lay their plans so they will be protected against these weaknesses. Real leaders do not merely surround themselves with a number of subordinates selected at random. They select with great care the person for the special job, later shifting and changing staff from one job to another whenever and wherever they find they have made a mistake.

Real leaders have a keen imagination and induce action on the part of followers by appealing to their imaginations. They do not rely upon their authority or power, nor do they try to instill fear in subordinates' hearts. Real leaders mainly rely upon an ability to sell their followers on doing what is most advantageous through presenting the advantages to them. They use persuasion, not power.

There are two types of leaders in the world. One resorts to power and controls followers through fear. The other resorts to persuasion and controls followers through able salesmanship. Individuals of the latter type are professional salespeople regardless of their calling. In warfare, leadership based upon power, authority, and fear may be essential, but in business, that form of leadership is despicable.

One reason Napoleon was the general of generals and the salesman of salesmen was that he used less fear and more motivation. The successful leader in business and industry induces people to do things because it is to their advantage to do them and not merely because he or she happens to be in power.

There are three types of motivation. The first, which is fear, is temporary. The second, incentive, is also temporary. The third, attitude, involves permanent change. Professional salespeople are essentially leaders, inducing people to cooperate in a spirit of harmony by planting adequate motives in their minds. They use persuasion instead of coercion; therefore their leadership endures. The professional salesperson reaches followers and influences them favorably through their emotions as well as their reason. All great leaders are professional salespeople, and all professional salespeople are great leaders.

They understand the art of persuasion. They understand how to set up in the minds of their followers motives which will induce favorable and willing cooperation.

Master salespeople can sell anything they choose to sell because they have sufficient initiative to create markets. Moreover, they can sell one commodity, idea, plan, service, or motive just as easily as any other. Professional salespeople are like great hunters. They shoot their game on the run, while others wait for someone to run their game by them. This is the type that usually comes home with no game.

Great leaders and professional salespeople use the same philosophy. They sell their followers or patrons whatever they choose to sell by establishing a relationship of confidence. One of the greatest leaders who ever lived stated the secret of his leadership in six words: "Kindness is more powerful than compulsion."

Chapter Nine

QUALIFYING THE
PROSPECTIVE BUYER

In the actual process of selling, the first step is to qualify the prospective buyer—that is, ascertaining tactfully from the prospect (and from other sources, if possible) the following information, which will be needed in presenting the sales plan:

1. How much money is the prospective purchaser prepared to spend, and how much should he or she be asked to spend?

2. Are conditions, including the prospective buyer's state of mind, favorable for closing the sale? If not, when are they likely to be?

3. Will the prospective buyer act for himself or herself, or must some lawyer, banker, wife, husband, relative, counselor, or other person be consulted before a deci-

sion can be reached? If so, who is the person to be consulted and for what specific purpose?

4. If the prospective buyer must consult another person before making a decision, will the salesperson be permitted to be present at the consultation? This is highly important. Salespeople cannot afford to have a third person to sit in judgment upon them and their products without being present to offer their own case.

5. Does the prospective buyer like to do most of the talking? If so, be sure to provide the opportunity. Every word a prospective buyer speaks will serve as a clue to what is in his or her mind. If prospective buyers are not inclined to talk freely, induce them to do so by asking questions that will bring out the desired information.

While qualifying prospective buyers, the salesperson will find it easy to ascertain just what alibi and what objections are likely to be offered when the closing point has been reached. The following are some of the most commonly used alibis to which practically all prospective buyers resort:

1. They will claim they do not have the money. The professional salesperson always takes this one with more than the proverbial grain of salt. If prospective buyers have been accurately qualified, the salesperson knows

their financial status and can therefore tactfully meet this objection.

2. The prospective buyer, if he is a man, may tell the salesperson that he does not wish to decide until he talks the matter over with his wife, banker, or lawyer. If he hides behind his wife's skirts, the professional salesperson will tactfully invite him to permit the salesperson to talk to the two of them together. At this interview, the professional will then analyze the wife and ascertain whether she is the real boss or is a mere alibi for her husband. If she is the boss, he will direct his sales efforts mainly to her.

3. Prospective buyers may claim they do not wish to reach a decision until they have had time to think the matter over. That is an old one. Professional salespeople know how much thinking the majority of people do about anything; however, in such cases, using tact, they will suggest ways and means of assisting the prospective buyer in the task of thinking. The professional salesperson permits prospective buyers to believe they are doing their own thinking, but takes care to see that they think with ideas and facts that the salesperson supplies.

This entire process of qualifying the prospective buyer must precede the attempt to close the sale. Practically every sale that is lost after the sales presentation has been made occurs for one of two reasons: the salesperson either has not properly neutralized the mind of the prospective buyer before the presentation, or has failed to accurately qualify the prospective buyer beforehand.

Professional salespeople never try to close a sale until they are absolutely sure they have painted in the prospective buyer's mind a picture that has created a strong desire for the products, and that the prospective buyer is able to buy them. This is a point on which no guessing should be done. It is professional salespeople's business to know. If they do not know, they are not professionals. Trying to sell a Mercedes to someone who has only a Ford income is wasted effort. Accurate qualification prevents such waste.

The first thing a professional salesperson asks a prospective purchaser of life insurance is, how much insurance do you now carry and what sort of policies do you have? Armed with this information, which is easily acquired for the asking, and knowing the prospective buyer's approximate financial status, the salesperson knows what policy to offer the client.

With the question method of qualifying prospective buyers, professional salespeople come prepared with a series of carefully thought out questions with which they acquire from their prospective purchasers such information as they need to qualify them accurately.

Most people will answer any reasonable questions asked of them. Care and thought in the presentation and asking of these questions will arm salespeople with all the information they need to close a sale. Moreover, the information will be authentic and reliable, because the prospect will supply it.

Let your prospect talk freely. When police officials arrest a man who is suspected of having committed a crime, they proceed immediately to induce him to talk. Every word he utters, as well as his refusal to talk on certain points, places in the hands of the investigators facts from which they can easily make important deductions.

Until the sales plan is actually presented, every professional salesperson is in reality an investigator. It is their business to get the facts, and the best method of getting them is to induce the prospective buyer to talk. Some who call themselves salespeople spoil their chances of making sales by opening their mouths and closing their eyes and ears.

The most successful salesperson manages an interview in such a tactful fashion that the prospective buyer believes *he* is managing it. When the sale has been closed, the buyer believes he or she has made a purchase rather than having been sold anything.

The most successful life insurance salesman in America specializes in the sale of life insurance policies to men with whom he plays golf. He takes great care, however, never to refer to his profession even briefly on the golf course. Moreover, he never tries to talk life insurance to his prospective buyers until after he has played golf with them at least three times. Even then he leads up to the subject through a series of cleverly prepared tactical questions, through which he induces his prospective buyers to ask him about life insurance. He calls himself a "life insurance counselor." It is his business, he tells prospective buyers, to go over their life insurance policies with them to ascertain whether or not they have the best form of insurance, the right amount, and so on. Naturally he chooses prospective buyers who carry large amounts of insurance and who therefore have many policies already in force. He has made hundreds of sales without asking his prospective buyers to take additional insurance, merely by analyzing their life insurance schedules in such a tactful way as to apply in their minds the thought that they need additional insurance of one sort or another.

Confidence is a condition of major importance, which must be created by professional salespeople in the minds of prospective buyers. If they qualify prospective buyers accurately, they build this confidence while doing so. No sale of note can be made without this element of confidence. Professional salespeople often stalk their prospective buyers for months while establishing confidence, meanwhile refraining from any attempt to make sales.

As for methods of qualifying, the skilled detective often plants stool pigeons where they can gain information about a suspect. Professional salespeople follow similar tactics, but they are their own stool pigeons and get the information firsthand. The nature of their work makes stealth in acquiring information unnecessary.

Sometimes, however, professional salespeople use skilled investigators, but they do not consider them to be stool pigeons. These investigators gather information about prospective buyers which the salespeople themselves cannot acquire in person. It is the professional salesperson's business, among other things, to get to know all about the prospective buyer—to get the facts.

Lobbyists, whose number in Washington is legion, often serve those who employ them more in the capacity of investigators than of salespeople. If they find anything in the private habits of a senator or a congressman that will not bear the spotlight of publicity, the discovery becomes valuable to their employers. The same tactics are employed with reference to other government officials, whose cooperation sometimes is sought on the basis of coercion rather than persuasion.

This form of qualification is reprehensible. Moreover, it is accompanied by great hazards to those who use it. This method of securing information is mentioned not with the object of recommending it, but in order to show

how important it is for those who seek to persuade others to have facts upon which to plan their presentations.

Salespeople who are too indifferent or too lazy to acquire sufficient facts to qualify prospective buyers deserve to fail, and usually do. Anyone is nine tenths beaten when an adversary gains possession of that person's motives and weaknesses, provided that the adversary has the intelligence to use the information effectively. Professional salespeople possess this intelligence. Indeed they become professional salespeople largely because of their ability to gather facts and to qualify accurately their prospective buyers.

When police officials are called in to solve a murder for which the motive is unknown, the first question they ask is, "Where is the woman in the case?" or they seek to determine whether a robbery was the motive. Unless the motive for the crime has been established, it is often difficult to apprehend the criminals or to convict them after they have been apprehended.

These are facts from which the professional salesperson may profit. Find out the prospective buyer's major motives and weaknesses, and the buyer is as good as in your bag before you begin.

Chapter Ten

NEUTRALIZING THE
PROSPECTIVE BUYER'S MIND

After prospective buyers have been qualified (or during the qualification process), their minds must be emptied of prejudice, bias, resentment, and all other conditions unfavorable to the salesperson. The prospective buyer's mind must be cultivated and prepared before the seed of desire can be successfully planted in it.

A neutral or favorable mind in a prospective buyer should contain, in the first place, *confidence*. The buyer must have confidence in the salesperson and in the product. In the second place, there must be *interest*. The buyer must be reached through an appeal to the imagination and interest aroused in the commodity offered for sale. Third is *motive*. The buyer must have a logical motive for buying. Building this motive is the salesperson's most important task. No prospective buyer's mind has been neutralized and made favorable until these three conditions exist in their mind.

The salesperson's first duty, then, is to create *confidence* in the mind of the prospective buyer. Obviously this cannot be done by arousing any negative emotions. It can only be done by a careful analysis of (1) the buyer; (2) the buyer's business or calling; (3) the obstacles that may face the buyer in the successful conduct of their business. Nothing builds confidence more quickly than a keen and genuine interest in the buyer's business problems.

There are four levels of human relationships: (1) closed mind; (2) open mind; (3) confidence; (4) belief. You can sell on the last two, but never on the first two. A person can slide from the fourth level, which is the highest, in one step, but must work up a step at a time.

There are ten major ways of building confidence:

1. Render more and better service then you are paid to render.
2. Enter into no transaction that does not benefit everyone it affects as nearly equally as possible.
3. Make no statement that you do not believe to be true, no matter what temporary advantages falsehood might seem to offer.
4. Have a sincere desire in your heart to be of the greatest possible service to the largest number of people.

5. Cultivate a wholesome admiration for people. Like them better than you like money.
6. Do your best to live as well as preach your own philosophy of business. Actions speak louder than words.
7. Accept no favors, large or small, without giving favors in return.
8. Ask nothing of any person without believing that you have a right to that for which you ask.
9. Enter into no arguments with any person over trivial or nonessential details.
10. Spread the sunshine of good cheer wherever and whenever you can. No one trusts a killjoy.

This list is well worth memorizing; it is also worth following.

A professional salesperson can sell someone anything they need if the purchaser has confidence in the salesperson. The salesperson can also sell people many things they do not need, but doesn't.

Remember, professional salespeople play the double role of buyer and seller. They therefore do not try to sell any person anything they themselves would not buy if they were in the position of the prospective buyer.

There is a well-known type of crook who is a professional salesman—the confidence man. His sole equipment is his ability to build confidence in the minds of his victims. His dealings run into the millions, and his victims may be found among the shrewdest of businesspeople, professionals, and bankers. These crooks often stalk their victims for months or even years for the purpose of building a relationship of perfect confidence. When this foundation has been properly laid, even the smartest individual may be taken in. People are without defense against those in whom they have perfect confidence.

If confidence can be used successfully as the crook's sole tool of operation, surely it can be used with greater effects for legitimate business and professional purposes. Salespeople who know how to build a bridge of confidence between themselves and their prospective purchasers may write their own income ticket, as all such salespeople do. High-pressure methods, exaggerated statements of facts, and willful misrepresentation, whether by direct statement or by innuendo, destroy confidence.

Some time ago, one of the biggest sales producers for a well-known automobile dealer was let out of his position. He was dismissed because a check of his accounts with the finance company disclosed the fact that more than three fourths of his customers had lapsed in their payments.

A further checkup disclosed the fact that this so-called salesman had high-pressured his buyers into signing orders by telling them that if anything happened that made it inconvenient for them to make their monthly payments promptly, they could skip a couple of months or so without jeopardizing their rights.

Through this man's acts, the automobile agency for which he worked lost prestige it will never be able to regain. Every successful business firm must have the confidence of its patrons. The salesperson is either the intermediary through which this confidence is acquired or the medium through which it is lost.

Professional salespeople, knowing as they do the importance of acquiring and holding the confidence of buyers, bargain with them as if they, the salespeople, were the owners of the business they represent. They deal with customers exactly as if they were owners of the business.

Confidence is the basis of all harmonious relationships. Salespeople who overlook this fact are unfortunate; they can never become professional salespeople. This means that they limit their earning capacity and circumscribe their possibilities of advancement.

At one point in Chicago, a professional salesman conducted a chain of men's hat stores. The hats were sold with a guarantee that if the customer found his purchase unsatisfactory, he could bring back the hat and receive a brand-new one in its place with no questions asked. One man had been coming back twice a year for more than seven years and exchanging his old hat for a new one.

"And you permit him to get away with that?" the owner was asked.

"Get away with it?" the store owner replied. "If I had a hundred men doing the same thing, I could retire from business with all the money I need inside of five years. Never a day passes that we do not trace sales to the talking done by this man. He is literally a walking and talking advertisement for us."

The statement throws an entirely different light on the subject. The owner had built an enormous business upon an unusual policy, which developed confidence.

There are two major occasions that cause men and women to talk and therefore advertise a business favorably or unfavorably: when they think they have been cheated and when they think they have received fairer treatment than expected. All people are like this. They are impressed by the law of contrast. Anything unusual or unexpected, whether it impresses favorably or unfavorably, makes a lasting impression.

Failure to neutralize the mind of the prospective buyer is one of the five major weaknesses of the majority of unsuccessful salespersons. There can be no fixed rule to be followed in neutralizing the minds of prospective buyers, as each individual case offers conditions peculiar to itself, and each case must be handled on its own merits. The salesperson with imagination will not be slow to recognize the most appropriate methods of approach for neutralizing the minds of prospective buyers.

Some methods that have been used successfully for sales preparation or neutralization are as follows:

1. *Social contacts through clubs.* It has been said that more business is done on the golf courses of America than in business offices. Certainly every supersalesperson knows the value of club contacts.

2. *Church affiliations.* Here one may make acquaintances without the usual formalities, under circumstances that tend to establish confidence.

3. *Lodge and union affiliations.* In many lines of selling, the salesperson will find it highly helpful to establish contacts through lodges and trade unions, where individuals naturally let down the bars of formality.

4. *Personal courtesies.* Dinner engagements offer a favorable opportunity to break down the resistance of formalities and to establish confidence.

5. *Personal service.* Under some conditions, salespeople are in a position to render valuable service and to supply helpful information to those with whom they intend to do business subsequently.

6. *Mutual interest and hobbies.* Nearly everyone has a hobby or some form of interest outside of their business or calling. When discussing or pursuing a hobby, one is always inclined to step out from the defense behind which one hides in the course of one's business routine.

The salesperson's second duty in preparing the mind of the prospect to receive favorably the seed of desire is to arouse *interest* in the product in the prospect's mind. This may require the application of one or all the qualities a master salesperson must possess, as has already been described. To arouse interest in the product, the salesperson will find it necessary to use imagination, faith, enthusiasm, knowledge of the merchandise, persistence, and showmanship. A neutral mind in the buyer will be of no advantage to the salesperson who lacks the ability to plant in the prospect's mind the seed of desire for the merchandise. That seed cannot be planted without interest upon the part of the prospect.

Finally, the salesperson must build the entire sales presentation around a central motive that is appropriate and suited to the business and financial status of the prospective buyer.

The three subjects of confidence, interest, and motive having been attended to, the salesperson has reached the point at which the sale may be closed. Scientific salesmanship involves principles similar to those upon which a successful stage play are based. The art of scientific salesmanship may be described as a three-act drama consisting of:

Act one: interest. This must be created by neutralizing the mind of the prospective buyer and establishing confidence.

Act two: desire. Desire must be developed through the proper presentation of motive.

Act three: action. Action, or the close, can be induced only by the proper presentation of the two preceding acts.

The psychology of selling an individual is closely akin to that used by actors in selling an audience. A successful stage play must have the advantage of a strong opening act and a smashing climax or closing act. If a play does not have these, it will be a flop. Act one must grip the attention and arouse the interest of the audience. Act two must develop the plot or presentation. Though this may be weak, it may yet go over, providing the first act has been strong. The audience (or buyers) will be charitable, providing they gain sufficient confidence from the first act to arouse expectations of a strong climax.

Act three must realize the objective. This must be a knockout, regardless of the first two acts, or the play will be a flop. The third or last act is where the sale is closed or lost.

Salespeople who fall down in the first act will experience difficulty if not impossibility in making a sale. The sales presentation may be weak at many places in the middle without fatality to the sale, providing the opening and the close are strong and impelling.

Obviously the director-salesperson who successfully presents the three-act drama of selling must possess and use imagination. Imagination is the workshop of the mind, which has fashioned every idea, plan, and mental picture with which the salesperson creates desire in the mind of the prospective buyer. Salespeople whose imaginations are deficient resemble a ship without a rudder. They go round and round in circles and finish where they started without making a favorable impression. Words alone will not sell. Words woven into combinations of thought that create desire *will* sell.

Some salespeople never learn the difference between rapid-fire conversation that does not end soon enough and carefully painted word pictures that fire the imagination of the prospective buyer.

Chapter Eleven

THE ART OF CLOSING A SALE

The climax or closing of a sale is said to be the most difficult part of the entire transaction. This is not true, however, if the groundwork leading up to the close has been properly laid. As a matter of fact, the climax is a mere detail if a sale has been properly made. In almost every instance when a sale is hard to close, the difficulty may be found in some part of the transaction preceding the climax.

As we have already seen, before trying to reach a climax, professional salespeople prepare the way carefully step-by-step through proper attention to the following important details:

1. They have taken care to neutralize the mind of the prospect, to make it receptive to the sales presentation.

2. They have made the mind of the prospect favorable by establishing confidence.

3. They have qualified the prospect accurately to make sure that they are dealing with a prospect and not a mere suspect.

4. Above all, they have planted in the prospect's mind the most logical motive for buying.

5. They have tested the prospect during the sales presentation and have made sure that the prospect followed the presentation with keen interest. This has been accomplished by keen observation of the prospect's facial expression and statements denoting a desire for the object of the sale.

6. Last, but by no means least, the salesperson has made the sale in their own mind before trying to reach a climax. They know this by the feel of the prospect's mind. No one can become a professional salesperson without developing the ability to tune in on the prospect's mind through the sixth sense. This ability, more than anything else, is the distinguishing feature of a professional salesperson.

Having taken these steps satisfactorily, the salesperson is now ready to close the sale. There are thousands of salespeople who can arouse interest, which is the first step in the process of selling. Creating a desire for their products is the second step, but at the third step, they fall down because they lack the ability to close.

Let it be remembered, however, that if the detailed steps described in this book have been properly taken, the close comes easily and is nothing but a mere detail.

The following suggestions will be helpful even to the seasoned salesperson in developing mastery in closing.

1. Do not permit your prospect to lead you away from your sales plan by engaging in argument over non-essentials or extraneous subjects. If your prospect insists upon breaking in while you're talking and tries to direct the conversation so as to build up a defensive alibi for not buying, let them go along until they exhaust themselves; then, the moment they hesitate, tactfully switch back to your own train of thought. Go right along and develop your own thoughts to the climax: this is absolutely essential. Either the salesperson or the prospect dominates. It makes a great difference to the sale which one does the dominating.

2. Anticipate negative questions and objections that you feel exist in the prospect's mind. Expose them to these questions; ask and answer them yourself. Never bring up negative questions unless you are sure that your prospect has them in mind; in selling, it pays to let sleeping dogs lie.

3. Always assume that your prospect is going to buy, no matter what they do or say to indicate the contrary, and let them know by every word and every movement that you expect them to buy. If you weaken on this point, you are beaten at the outset, because your buyer may be shrewd enough to observe that you are not sure of yourself. If they do, they will use this as an alibi with which to give you a negative answer when you try to close. The professional salesperson never wavers for a moment and never shows the white feather, regardless of how clever the prospect may be at setting traps for this purpose. Some prospects are quite as clever at leading the salesperson off the scent as the professional salesperson is at sticking to the trail of the argument. Be on the lookout for this sort of tactic, and be prepared to negotiate successfully through opposition of this nature.

4. Assume the attitude that your buyer is right: that they know their business. Any suggestion that you make, by direct statement or by innuendo, that you are smarter than the prospect will be sure to antagonize them, although they may not show their antagonism openly. The majority of mediocre salespeople make the mistake of trying to impress their prospects with their own superior knowledge. This is usually poor salesmanship. It has lost more than one opportunity for making a sale.

5. When naming the amount of the purchase, set the figure high. It is better to come down in the amount (if you find that necessary) than it is to set the amount too low and then find yourself with no margin on which to trade when closing time comes. Even if the figure you name is out of the prospect's financial range, your assumption of their ability to buy at the larger amount will not offend them. If, however, you make the mistake of underestimating their financial ability, you may offend. It has happened many times.

6. Use the question method to induce your prospect to commit themselves on vital points out of which you intend to build your sales presentation, then refer to those points as their own ideas. This is one of the most effective sales tactics, since people will naturally uphold any statement they have made or think they have made.

7. If your prospective buyer says they wish to consult their banker, lawyer, spouse or some acquaintance whose opinion they value, congratulate them on their good judgment and exercise of caution, then tactfully suggest that while bankers may know the moneylending business, lawyers may understand the technicalities of a law, and wives and friends may be well informed and loyal, the fact still remains that not one of them is apt to know as much about the product you are offering as you yourself know. You

have all the facts, while others have not, and they are not apt to take sufficient time or have sufficient interest to procure them. Moreover, plant the thought in the prospect's mind that after all, they know their own mind and their own business better than any other person.

8. Avoid permitting your prospects to think the matter over unless they have a very logical reason for the delay. When they spring that sort of alibi, pin them down and help them do the necessary thinking right then and there. An ounce of persistence at this point is worth a ton of cure afterward. The truth is, most sales which are lost could have been saved had the salesman been persistent for a few minutes longer.

Much has been said about closing sales at the psychological moment, but experience has shown that the majority of salespeople do not know when it is. The psychological moment is the time when the salesperson feels that the prospect is ready to close. There is such a moment in every sale, whether it be consummated or not. One of the major differences between a professional salesperson and a mediocre one is the professional's ability to sense what is in the prospect's mind aside from what the prospect has expressed in actual words. The mediocre salesperson lacks keenness of perception through the sixth sense.

When you sense the psychological moment for closing, name the amount involved in the purchase and proceed to close the transaction right then. A delay of a few minutes, and often even a few seconds, may give the prospect a chance to change their mind. If, when you try to close your sale, you find that you have misjudged the psychological moment, go back over your sales presentation again, bringing in new closing arguments that you have saved for just such an emergency. You will need quite a stock of emergency arguments if you are to be placed in the category of professional salespeople. No professional salesperson ever uses all of their trump cards unless they are forced to do so. Even then, they do not use them all at one time. They hold some back in case they have to make a secondary sales presentation to get the order.

The psychological moment for closing is something the salesperson usually has to sense, although there are times when the moment is obvious, either from the statements of the prospect or from their facial expression. The salesperson whose mind is negative or who is lacking in self-confidence often misses the feel of the psychological moment for closing, mistaking their own state of mind for that of their prospect.

On the other hand, this principle works in another way that is very advantageous for the sale. The prospect often mistakes the salesperson's positive mind, self-confidence, and assurance for the prospect's own willingness to buy and acts accordingly if the salesperson insists upon closing the sale. If salespeople can transmit negative thoughts to prospective buyers—which they most assuredly can and do if they are not professionals—they can also transmit positive thoughts.

Herein may be found the real reason why the salesperson should always assume an attitude both in manner and thought of belief that a sale will be consummated. Eagerness to close a sale hurriedly, if observed by the prospective buyer, is generally fatal, because it is always accompanied by a lack of confidence on the part of the salesperson, who transmits their own thought to the mind of the prospect. In fact, the salesperson may have already disclosed their state of mind by their words and facial expression. If the prospect gets the impression, no matter how, that the salesperson is eager to make a sale because they need the profit from the sale, the chance of making the sale is usually spoiled. A salesperson who carries an air of prosperity and nonchalance, reflected in personal appearance and tone of voice, is usually a successful closer. The reason is obvious.

Professionals seldom ask prospects if they are ready to close. They go right ahead and at the psychological moment make up the order, conducting themselves in every way as if the question of the sale were settled. Asking prospects if they are ready to close is the equivalent of expressing doubt that they are, but making up the order and handing it to the prospective buyer leaves no doubt as to the salesperson's state of mind on this subject. The buyer usually acts favorably upon such a positive suggestion, provided, of course, that the sales presentation has been properly made and the desire to buy has been planted in the prospect's mind.

Remember that a salesperson first closes a sale in his or her own mind. The whole world stands aside and makes room for individuals who know exactly what they want and have made up their minds to have just that. Those who hesitate, and by that hesitation express lack of confidence, will find that the crowd will walk all over their toes. When closing time comes, doubters may as well not ask for the order; they are almost certain to meet with a refusal. This is the way that human minds work.

When do you close—at the start, in the middle, or at the finish? All three are right, for the close should be a smooth, uninterrupted sequence, chosen by the prospect, who is giving you buying signals.

It is important that one be able to realize where a sale potentially exists and follow to successful conclusion situations that might not have been obvious sales opportunities.

A car salesman once committed a cardinal but common sin in sales. Late one afternoon, just before closing time, a young couple walked into the salesroom and told him they were interested in a car. Because the salesman had already prejudged them as owing more money on their old car than it would bring, he hurriedly excused himself in order to catch the next customer.

Did they buy? Yes, not only one but two cars. The salesman later learned that the wife's dad was a banker and had promised them a new car for Christmas. Her car was paid for, so a second salesman, the one who actually worked with them, quickly suggested that they buy two new cars. It is never a good idea to prejudge a prospect.

Another story: One man sent out word to several real estate agents that he was in the market for property in the country and described in detail the sort of place he wanted.

Salespeople came by the score. That they were all hungry for business was plainly indicated by their eagerness to put the man on the spot. Most of them described their properties by showing him maps and printed literature and asking him to look these over and let them know when he was ready to see the property. How did they know he was not then ready? Not one of them had the initiative to invite him out to see their property, with the exception of one, who was perhaps the only real salesman who showed up.

This salesman said, "We have just the place your letter described. We've been holding it for a long time," winking to show the man that he was taking a slight liberty with his credulity. "Jump in my car, and we'll run out and see your property. If it is not exactly what you want, I'll buy you the best dinner in the city when we return. When you see this place, you will look no further. I'm sure it is just what you want."

By that time, the prospective purchaser had begun to believe the salesman knew what he wanted, and he did something he had not intended to do, namely to inspect the property that day. The salesman's whole demeanor was so positive and assured that the client found himself in his car before he had a chance to think of a good reason for not going. If the salesman had hesitated in his approach, the client could have put him off until the following day, but it was his business to strike while the iron was hot.

On the way, this salesman described the place so accurately and so pleasingly that the man almost felt himself the owner of it before he had seen it. The salesman had planted the seed of desire in the man's mind so deeply that he was like putty in his hands.

The salesman took a contract with him and got the buyer's name on the dotted line before they left the property. The moment the salesman sensed that the man was ready to sign, he took out his contract and handed it to him with his pen. When the man said he had nothing to rest the contract on while signing, the salesman rushed to his car and pulled out a briefcase, saying, "Here, use this for a table."

This salesman handed the buyer no literature to read over; he handed him the property instead. Professional salespeople always do something like that. It is one of their peculiarities.

Later one of the other realtors came in to see the man, wanting to know if he had made up his mind about that country place he was looking for.

"Bless your life, yes," the man replied. "Perhaps I should say, however, that I did not make up my mind to buy it. A very able salesman made it up for me the same day that you first came to see me and made the sale that very day."

"That's too bad!" the salesman exclaimed.

"No," the man replied. "It is only one bad. It may be bad for you, but it was just fine for me, because I got the place I was looking for."

This dilatory salesman turned and walked away without saying good-bye.

You cannot tell how far a frog can jump by counting the warts on his back. No more can you tell by merely looking at a prospect whether you can sell them your product. Give yourself the benefit of the doubt and give every prospect the works before registering a no sale in your own mind. It is the safest plan.

Once a sales army of twenty-five hundred men and women had to be trained for a Dallas firm. Efficiency had to be the watchword. The trainers inaugurated a system that shows a great deal about the possibilities of persistence. Before any salesperson was permitted to become permanently allied with the organization, it was necessary for them to sell one out of the first five prospective buyers they called on. The instructions were to stick to these five prospects until a sale had been made. One salesman called a prospect eighteen times before he made a sale. The victim succumbed on the eighteenth visit and made a purchase out of self-defense. In the group of twenty-five hundred salespeople, only 113 failed to qualify for permanent positions because they could not make a sale to the first five prospects called on. These salespeople learned that *no* seldom need be taken seriously.

It was also apparent that confidence must be manifested by the salesperson as well as by the prospect before a sale can be effected. To make sure that the salespeople acquired confidence, the trainers resorted to a unique plan: that of setting up dummy offices maintained by the company and managed by company employees. When they felt sure that a green salesperson lacked only the quality of self-confidence, they included in the list of the first five prospects the name of one of these dummy managers, who was instructed to give the salesperson a hard battle, but to let them win by making a sale. These sales went through, and commissions were paid on them.

The effect was astounding, especially in the cases of salespeople who had never tried to sell before. The salesperson usually had to call on the dummy buyer last, after the four legitimate prospects had been called on. It turned out that the sale to the dummy was so encouraging that the trainers could then send the salespeople back to the list of the four who had not been sold, with a result that in some instances, all four of them were sold, despite the previous failures.

This experiment shows that the salesperson's state of mind has more to do with determining whether a sale is made than the state of mind of the prospective buyer. It is an important discovery.

Although this has been a varied and detailed examination of the subject of selling, the concept could be summed up in one word. This word should stand out upon the horizon of every salesperson's vision like Mars blazing at eventide—always there to be seen, challenging, beckoning, urging, inspiring, commanding. The word denotes the thing that dominates all great and able salespeople everywhere, and it is a word that has been called the greatest in the English language. It is *service*. If you are successful, remember that somewhere, sometime, someone gave you a lift or an idea that started you in the right direction. Remember also that you are indebted to life until you help some less fortunate person, just as you have been helped.

Printed in the USA
CPSIA information can be obtained
at www.ICGtesting.com
JSHW012036140824
68134JS00033B/3086

9 781722 503093